Perfect Letters and Emails for All Occasions

George Davidson is a former senior editor with Chambers Harrap. He is an experienced researcher, writer and editor of reference books, and has written two other books in the *Perfect* series. He lives in Edinburgh.

Other titles in the *Perfect* series

Perfect Answers to Interview Questions – Max Eggert
Perfect Babies' Names – Rosalind Fergusson
Perfect Best Man – George Davidson
Perfect Brain Training – Philip Carter
Perfect Calorie Counting – Kate Santon
Perfect Confidence – Jan Ferguson
Perfect CV – Max Eggert
Perfect Detox – Gill Paul
Perfect Family Quiz – David Pickering
Perfect Interview – Max Eggert
Perfect Memory Training – Fiona McPherson
Perfect Numerical Test Results – Joanna Moutafi and Ian Newcombe
Perfect Numerical and Logical Test Results – Joanna and Marianna Moutafi
Perfect Party Games – Stephen Curtis
Perfect Personality Profiles – Helen Baron
Perfect Persuasion – Richard Storey
Perfect Positive Thinking – Lynn Williams
Perfect Presentations – Andrew Leigh and Michael Maynard
Perfect Psychometric Test Results – Joanna Moutafi and Ian Newcombe
Perfect Pub Quiz – David Pickering
Perfect Punctuation – Stephen Curtis
Perfect Readings for Weddings – Jonathan Law
Perfect Relaxation – Elaine van der Zeil
Perfect Speeches for All Occasions – Matt Shinn
Perfect Wedding Planning – Cherry Chappell
Perfect Wedding Speeches and Toasts – George Davidson
Perfect Weight Loss – Kate Santon
Perfect Written English – Chris West

Perfect
Letters and Emails
for All Occasions

George Davidson

BOOKS

Published by Random House Books 2010

10 9 8 7 6 5 4 3 2 1

First published in the United Kingdom in 2010 by
Random House Books

Random House,
20 Vauxhall Bridge Road,
London SW1V 2SA

www.rbooks.co.uk

Addresses for companies within The Random House Group Limited
can be found at: www.randomhouse.co.uk/offices.htm

The Random House Group Limited Reg. No. 954009

A CIP catalogue record for this book
is available from the British Library

ISBN 9781847945495

The Random House Group Limited supports The Forest Stewardship
Council® (FSC®), the leading international forest-certification organisation.
Our books carrying the FSC label are printed on FSC®-certified paper.
FSC is the only forest-certification scheme supported by the leading
environmental organisations, including Greenpeace. Our
paper procurement policy can be found at
www.randomhouse.co.uk/environment

MIX
Paper | Supporting
responsible forestry
FSC® C018179

Typeset by Palimpsest Book Production Limited, Grangemouth, Stirlingshire

Printed and bound in Great Britain by Clays Ltd, St Ives plc

Contents

Quick Reference Section

Introduction

Letter-writing is not as important as it once was. Many of the functions fulfilled by letters in times past are now handled by telephone calls, emails or even text messages. Nevertheless, in some situations and for some purposes only a letter will do.

Many people, however, have little experience of letter-writing nowadays, and faced with the need to write, say, wedding invitations, a job application or perhaps a complaint about faulty goods, they are not sure how to set about it – what to write, how to express it, and how to set out the letter on the page. And, of course, there are the letters that everyone finds difficult, such as expressions of condolence. Don't you so often wish there was someone you could turn to for help in finding the right words to say?

Whatever the situation you find yourself in, whatever the letter you need to write, you will find the answers to your questions in this book. Nothing is taken for granted. *Perfect Letters and Emails* starts with the basics of how to set out a letter and address an envelope, and then moves on to general advice on how to draft, write and check your letter, before taking you chapter by chapter through the various types of letter you may have to write. Along with many specimen letters that you can adapt to suit your own situation and requirements (and your own style and personality), there are discussions of do's and don'ts, of what to say and what not to, so that you can confidently create the letters you need.

As the title suggests, this book deals not only with letters but also with emails – discussing, for example, when you might send an email instead of a letter and when it would not be appropriate to do so, and how emails differ from letters in form and style. In addition, in the chapter on business letters we will have a few words to say about office memos, and in the chapter on employment-related letters we will cover not only the letters or emails you might need to write but also the preparation of your curriculum vitae.

If you are writing to a member of the government, the nobility or the clergy, it is important to address them correctly both in your letter and on the envelope. For that reason, you will find at the end of this book a Quick Reference guide to correct forms of address.

And finally, since no letter or email can be perfect if it contains spelling mistakes, bad grammar or poor punctuation, you should study carefully the 'Watch your language!' section on pages 184 to 202, where the worst and most frequent errors are pointed out and corrected.

If you find letter-writing a chore, this book will certainly make writing letters easier for you. But perhaps more importantly, it will also ensure that your letters are pleasing to read and communicate effectively what you want to say, and are therefore likely to achieve the results you are hoping for.

I would like to thank Sophie Lazar and Gemma Wain for their assistance and advice during the preparation of this book.

NOTE: All names and addresses in the letters and emails are invented, and any resemblance to actual people, companies or addresses is entirely coincidental.

1 Letter structure and layout

A perfect letter must be properly laid out, pleasing to look at and easy to read. There are a number of conventions concerning structure and layout, especially important in formal or business letters, which this chapter will explain and illustrate.

There are two main types of letter layout you need to be familiar with:

- the **indented** layout, and
- the **blocked** layout.

Indented letter layout

Here is an example of an informal handwritten letter set out in an indented layout:

47 Ashby Gardens,
Woltonborough,
CT27 4XQ

27/10/10

Dear Mary,
   I've been meaning to write to you for absolutely ages, so now the children are in bed (Jim is out at the gym as usual on a Wednesday night), I am going to sit down and bring you up to date with all our news.

I don't remember if I told you that I was thinking of going back to work now that Jamie and Susie are both at school. Well, I'm back at the bank again! Only for three days a week, though. I think that's enough at the moment, and I wouldn't want to give up my Thursday afternoon badminton! It's the only real exercise I get these days.

Do you remember Anna Murray? I met her by chance the other day in the supermarket . . .

[This letter would be too long to print in full. So let's move on to the end.]

Well, that's all my news for now. Do write soon and let me know how you and Adam are getting on. No sign of a baby yet? Or are you still too busy to think of starting a family?

> *Love,*
> *Joanne*

The address

In an indented letter layout, you put your address in the top right-hand corner of the page, beginning anywhere to the right of the midpoint of the page. (Exactly where you start your address line will depend on the length of your address: obviously '20 Ash Lane' could start further to the right than '20 Cambridge Racecourse Crescent'.)

How much of your address you choose to put in depends on how well the person you are writing to knows you. For close friends and relatives who know your address perfectly well, it is unnecessary to write it out in full. A shorter version, such as

> *47 Ashby Gardens,*
> *Woltonborough*

or even just one or other of these lines, would be enough. But in letters to people you are less well acquainted with, write out your full address.

Each line of the address starts slightly to the right of the beginning of the line above. If your house has a name, it may stand as the first line of the address:

> *Ash Cottage,*
> *47 Ashby Gardens,*
> *Woltonborough*

Give the house number even if giving the house name.

Punctuation

There is no punctuation at the end of the last line of the address. Many people prefer to put commas at the end of the other lines, especially in handwritten letters, but they are not essential. There is no need for a comma between the house number and the street name.

Telephone number, etc

Other information, such as your telephone number and/or your email address, can be put below your address (aligned with the first line) or in the top left-hand corner of your letter, depending on what looks best on the size of paper you are using:

> *47 Ashby Gardens,*
> *Woltonborough*
> *Tel: 01234 897654*
> *Email: jojim47@anisp.co.uk*

or

Tel: 01234 897654   *47 Ashby Gardens,*
Email: jojim47@anisp.co.uk   *Woltonborough*

Do not cram your address and other information into the top corner or corners of the page; your letter will look better if you leave some space as a top margin. And if you are writing a short letter on a large sheet of paper, bring the address down even further on the page so that the whole letter will be more balanced towards the centre of the sheet.

The date

The date should come below your address, with a little space between it and the address (a one- or two-line space if you are typing your letter), and should be aligned with the first line of the address, as in the letter above.

There are various acceptable ways of writing the date, such as:

27 October 2010 or *27th October 2010* (no comma needed)
October 27th, 2010 (with a comma)
27 Oct 10 or *27-Oct-10* or *27/10/10* or *27.10.10*

If you want to include the day of the week, these are styles you could use:

Wednesday, 27th October 2010 (with one comma)
Wednesday, October 27th, 2010 (with two commas)

Of course you could use shorter forms if you want to, e.g.:

Wed 27 Oct 10 (with even the comma after *Wed* omitted)

Avoid ambiguous dates

Remember that there are different date conventions in different parts of the world: in British English 7/10/10 = 7th October 2010, whereas in America 7/10/10 = 10th July 2010. If there is any possibility of confusion, write the date in an unambiguous form.

Headed notepaper

If you are using headed notepaper, the printed address will often be centred on the page. In this case, you should write the date at the left-hand side of the page, not under the address:

47 ASHBY GARDENS
WOLTONBOROUGH
CT27 4XQ

27th October 2010

The salutation

The salutation is the first short line of the letter, in which you address the person or people you are writing to. It begins in line with the left-hand side of the text of the letter, lower than the date line by about a one- or two-line space, generally starts with the word 'Dear', and is followed by a comma:

Tel: 01234 897654   *47 Ashby Gardens,*
Email: jojim47@anisp.co.uk   *Woltonborough*
                                         CT27 4XQ

                                         27/10/10

Dear Mary,

The word 'Dear' is of course purely conventional, and does not necessarily imply any close relationship with or affection for the person you are writing to. A slightly more intimate and informal salutation would be:

My dear Mary or *My dear Mrs Carter*

In a letter to a loved one you could write something even more intimate, such as:

Dearest Elizabeth or *My dearest John* or *My darling Joyce*

(though this might not be to everyone's taste).

Round-robin letters

If you are sending out the same letter to many people, for example along with Christmas cards, you could omit the salutation, but it is more friendly if you add a general greeting such as 'Dear family and friends' or 'Dear fellow members of Brownbank Bowling Club'.

The body of the letter

In the indented layout, each paragraph, including the first one, begins a few spaces in from the left-hand margin. Since the start of each new paragraph is indicated by the indentation, you do not need to leave a line space between paragraphs. However, many people choose to do so, especially in typed letters, and an extra line inserted between paragraphs can be useful if you want to spread out a short letter to fill more of a large page.

If you are using a computer, you could automatically justify the lines of your letter (that is, make them all the same length), but it is better not to do so in informal letters. Justified lines give a letter a rather formal appearance; unjustified lines of different lengths look friendlier.

Margins

How much clear space you leave around your letter, if any, is up to you. Do whatever will make your letter look good on the page. Computer printers are usually set to automatically leave a margin at the top and bottom of the page and at both sides, though you can alter these settings to suit yourself.

The complimentary close

The complimentary close is the phrase you use to round off your letter, such as 'Yours sincerely' or 'With best wishes', followed by your name.

Leave a line space between the end of your letter (more or less a line in a handwritten letter) and the complimentary close, which should be indented as far in from the left-hand margin as the beginning of a paragraph (or even closer to the centre of the page if you prefer).

Follow the complimentary word or phrase with a comma, and then write your name on the next line, slightly to the right again. In a business letter you should type your name below your signature for the sake of clarity:

I hope this matter can be resolved quickly.

Yours sincerely,

[signature here]

Geoffrey Wilson

Punctuation

If you write something like 'With love from' or 'Best wishes from' in your complimentary close, there should be no comma after the 'from'.

Only the first word of the complimentary close has a capital letter, e.g.:

Yours sincerely not *Yours Sincerely*

Never have the complimentary close and your signature alone on the last page of a letter. Always space your letter out so that there is at least a line or two of the last paragraph above the complimentary close.

Your signature

Even if you have typed your letter, you should nevertheless always *write* your name. Blue or black ink is best if you are writing a formal letter; other colours might seem a bit frivolous.

If your signature is not clear and easily readable, type or print your name below it (always do so in a business letter). And if you have a name that does not clearly indicate your sex, it is helpful to the recipient of your letter if you put '(Mr)' or '(Mrs)' or whatever after your name to avoid any uncertainty.

The recipient's address

Since letters in indented layout tend to be informal rather than business letters (which are usually written in the blocked style described below), it is not usually necessary to include the name and address of the person you are writing to. But if you are handwriting a business letter, you may choose to use an indented layout, in which case the recipient's name and address should be included, aligned with the left-hand margin, above the salutation:

47 Ashby Gardens,
Woltonborough,
CT27 4XQ

2 December 2010

The Manager,
Bucks Bank plc,
66 Ryle Road,
Milton Newbury,
MN31 3HR

Dear Sir,
. . . . . .

Leave at least a line space below the date and a line space above the salutation. (You can add more space in order to spread a short text over a large page.)

Blocked letter layout

Here is an example of a typed letter in blocked style:

> *23 Rosewood Gardens*
> *Romerton*
> *PM10 3RS*
>
> *14 September 2010*

Anis Printer Supplies
South Bank Industrial Estate
Portavon
TS23 8QT

Dear Sirs,

Order Number 10/67153

I ordered from you on 10 September two cartridges of black toner for a Takto printer TK1005.

I understood that, while the toner cartridges you would supply would not be actual Takto products, they would nevertheless be compatible with a Takto printer. However, I have found this not to be the case. When I loaded one of your cartridges into my printer, a warning flashed up indicating that the cartridge was incompatible with it. The same thing happened with the second cartridge.

I have now bought a genuine Takto toner cartridge, and have had no problems with it. The fault would therefore seem to be with your own toner cartridges, which appear to be not in fact compatible with my printer.

I am therefore returning the cartridges to you and would be grateful if you would refund the money paid for them within the next fourteen days.

Yours faithfully,

[signature here]

Thomas Sheridan

As far as the content of the letter (address, date, salutation, complimentary close, etc) is concerned, the blocked letter has essentially the same structure as the indented letter style. The two styles of layout differ only in the look of the page.

In a blocked letter layout, nothing is indented. The lines of the sender's address and the date are all aligned, although still placed on the right-hand side of the page (unless you are using headed paper, in which case the address will possibly be centred on the page). All other parts of the letter are aligned with the left-hand margin.

Since new paragraphs are not indicated by indentation, you should leave a line space between each paragraph.

In keeping with the modern trend towards minimum punctuation, there are no commas at the end of lines in addresses. Some people also omit the commas after the salutation and the complimentary close, which is quite acceptable.

Variations on the blocked style

- The address and date may be completely aligned with the right-hand margin:

23 Rosewood Gardens
Romerton
PM10 3RS

14 September 2010

- The address and date may be aligned with the left-hand margin:

23 Rosewood Gardens
Romerton
PM10 3RS

14 September 2010

Dear Sirs,

However, aligning everything with the left-hand margin can give your letter a rather unbalanced look, especially if you are including both your address and the recipient's address.

- The date may be placed below the recipient's address:

23 Rosewood Gardens
Romerton
PM10 3RS

Anis Printer Supplies
South Bank Industrial Estate
Portavon
TS23 8QT

14 September 2010

Dear Sirs,

While this is quite acceptable, it is perhaps more logical to have the recipient's name and address immediately before the salutation rather than separated from it.

- The complimentary close may be placed more centrally on the page, as in the indented layout, to give the page more balance:

I look forward to hearing from you.

Yours faithfully,

[signature here]

Thomas Sheridan

In all these minor details of layout, choose the form you personally prefer.

Subject lines

If a letter needs a heading or subject line that briefly indicates the subject matter of the letter, this should follow the salutation. Leave a line space below the salutation and a line space between the subject line and the text of the letter. In a blocked letter layout the subject line is aligned with the left-hand margin, as in the letter above. In an indented letter layout, centre the heading on the page:

Dear Sirs,

<u>Order Number 10/67153</u>

I ordered from you on 10 September two cartridges of . . .

The heading should be underlined (or you could put it in **boldface** type if you are typing the letter on a computer).

The writer's position or status

It is often helpful, especially in a formal or business letter, for letter-writers to state their position or status. If you do this, add the information below your signature, in parentheses if you prefer, and split over two lines if necessary for balance:

> *Yours faithfully,*
>
> [signature here]
>
> *Peter Smith*
> *(Secretary, Luton Branch,*
> *World Aid Association)*

References

The headings of business letters may include company references of the sender, of the recipient, or of both. These are generally placed above the date:

> *Anis Printer Supplies*
> *South Bank Industrial Estate*
> *Portavon*
> *TS23 8QT*

Your ref: JA/GD
Our ref: FT-110810

11 August 2010

Erskine Henderson plc,
26 North Esk Street,
. . . . . .

Use of indented and blocked layouts

The indented layout is the one you would normally use for informal or slightly formal letters, especially if they are handwritten. The blocked layout is the one you would normally use for business letters, especially if they are typed. Quite simply, it looks more businesslike.

2 What to write on and what to write with

For the time being we will assume that you are writing or printing out on paper, although of course many letters can be sent as emails (see Chapter 4).

Informal letters

- Informal letters are equally acceptable handwritten or typed. If your handwriting is difficult to read, though, you might opt for typing. Letters expressing **congratulations**, **thanks**, **condolences** or **apologies** are generally better handwritten, however, to add a personal or more intimate touch.

- Whether writing or typing your letter, you should choose paper of a good quality rather than, for example, simply tearing a sheet of paper out of a notebook. A scrappy sheet of paper with torn edges looks really terrible, and will make a bad impression on the recipient of your letter. You could also use notelets for handwritten or typed letters.

- The best colours of paper to choose are white or a pale colour such as cream or ivory.

- Plain unlined paper generally looks better than lined paper. If you are writing your letter by hand and you need help in keeping your writing straight on the page, then buy a pad of paper that includes a lined guide sheet which you can slip under the page you are writing on and follow to keep your lines straight.

- Always write in pen, not pencil. While perhaps there is nothing to beat a good fountain pen or cartridge pen, a ballpoint pen is perfectly acceptable nowadays so long as it flows smoothly. Do not use felt-tip pens, though, as they could give your letters a rather childish appearance.

- Dark blue and black are the best colours of ink to use, as they are the easiest to read on white or pale-coloured paper.

- If you are typing your letter, choose a plain and easily readable typeface. Don't use fancy or florid typefaces, which are not easy to read and not appropriate for most letter-writing. (*Would you want to read a long letter in a typeface like this? Neither would I. It's rather hard on the eyes.*) Print in black; any other colour would be unexpected and therefore probably inappropriate.

In very informal chatty letters you might write to close friends and family, most of the above conventions do not apply. You can use any type, size or colour of paper you like, and any colour of ink, or even pencil or felt-tip pen. Use any typeface that appeals to you – but remember that some are hard to read even if attractive to look at.

Additional points to note

- It is perfectly acceptable to write or print an informal letter on both sides of the page (whereas a business letter should always be on only one side of the paper).

- Many people like to number the pages or sheets of their letters. This seems unnecessary in a short letter, but it is quite a sensible practice in longer letters in case the sheets get out of order.

- If you are writing to someone whose eyesight is not good, remember to write or print in letters large enough for them to read comfortably.

Business letters

- Business letters should be typed if possible, and printed in black ink. If handwritten, they should be in black or blue ink, using a good-quality pen.

- They should be written or printed on good-quality white paper.

- They should be written or printed on only one side of the paper.

- When printing business letters from a computer, it is wise to follow the official recommendation of using 12-point as your print size; however, if you feel that 12-point is rather large, 11-point is acceptable. Nothing smaller than that will do, though.

- A sans serif typeface (that is, one like this in which the letters do not have tiny decorative strokes at their tips) is also often recommended as being easier to read than a serif typeface (one that has the little decorative strokes). However, many people prefer the look of a serif typeface.

- Business letters should be signed in blue or black ink.

Paper size

If writing your letter by hand, choose a sheet size appropriate to the length of your letter. This will depend both on the size of your handwriting and on the amount of material you have to include in the letter; for example, a short letter written in small handwriting would look very unbalanced if it was written at the top of a large sheet of paper, whereas a long letter in large writing could look rather clumsy if written on several small sheets of paper.

> It is a good idea to have more than one size of notepaper to hand, so that you can choose a sheet or sheets of suitable dimensions for any particular letter. In letter-writing, one size really doesn't fit all.

If you are printing your letter from a computer, you will almost certainly be using the standard A4 size of paper regardless of how long or short your letter is; take care over how you set out your letter so that it looks as well-balanced as possible.

Planning ahead

If you are writing a letter by hand, work out in advance how long (at least approximately) it is likely to be, and therefore how much of a page or how many pages you think it will cover. Then . . .

- if you have a choice, choose an appropriate size of paper;

- if you have no choice, consider how to spread your text over the page to give it a balanced look, by for example using large margins and increasing the amount of space between your address, the date, the salutation, etc.

3 Envelopes

Envelopes come in various shapes, sizes and colours, and you should choose the right envelope for the job:

- It is best to use an envelope that matches the colour and quality of the paper. For letters of any type, it is best not to use brown envelopes. Brown envelopes are, however, perfectly acceptable for other types of business communication (for example, for sending out invoices and receipts).

- Choose a size and shape of envelope that will not require you to fold your letter more than twice. You don't want too many folds in a letter: it can make it difficult to open flat for reading.

> For business letters, envelopes are usually C4 (for A4 sheets flat), C5 (for A4 sheets folded once) and DL (for A4 sheets folded into three) sizes. Envelopes for personal correspondence come in a variety of sizes to match the size of the notepaper being used. The Royal Mail recommended minimum size for an envelope is 140 × 90 mm.

Reusing envelopes

In these waste-conscious times, many people reuse envelopes by means of stick-on labels which cover the old address and allow a new one to be written on top. This is laudable, but not always appropriate. You might well reuse an envelope in this way when writing to friends and family, perhaps even to your local councillor or MP, but you would be unwise to do so when posting something more formal and businesslike such as a job application. First impressions are important and you cannot be sure what impression a reused envelope might make on the recipient of your letter.

Addressing an envelope

Since the purpose of writing an address on an envelope is to enable the letter to be delivered to the person or company you are sending it to, the address has to be written clearly enough on the envelope to be easily and accurately deciphered, whether by human being or machine. The following points should be noted:

- The address should be written or printed parallel to the long side of the envelope.

- Write the address clearly. If your handwriting is not easily readable, type and print out the address, using a clear plain typeface. Do not use italics. As with the text of letters (see page 19), 11- or 12-point is a good size of print to use, but anything between 10- and 15-point is acceptable. It is also worth bearing in mind that most of the typefaces recommended by the Royal Mail and other countries' postal services are 'sans serif' (see page 19).

- Take care to write the house or building number correctly, and make sure you correctly name the street (is it 'Road', 'Street', 'Drive', 'Avenue', etc?).

- The main postal town or city name should be in capital letters.

- Make sure that the colour of the ink used for the address stands out clearly against the colour of the envelope. The colour of the address should be darker than the colour of the envelope, not the other way round.

- Position the address on the envelope so that it will not be obscured by the stamp, postage label or postmark.

- Begin the first line of the address at a point that will allow you to write the full address clearly without it becoming cramped. A clear 5 mm margin round the address is recommended.

- If you are using a window envelope, make sure that the whole address is clearly visible through the window, and that the letter inside is folded in such a way that it won't move about and hide the address.

- For a business letter, include if possible both the name and (on the next line) the title of the recipient and/or their department. You can also write 'For the attention of' or 'FAO' on the envelope above or beside the name.

- If you are writing to someone privately at their business address, put 'Private & Confidential' at the top left-hand corner of the envelope, so that your letter will not be opened by a secretary or PA.

- If writing to a member of the clergy, of the nobility or of the government, take care to address the envelope correctly. (See Quick Reference 2, page 173.)

Indented and blocked address layouts

As with letters, addresses on envelopes can be either indented or blocked:

> *Mrs J Carter,*
> *16 Abbey Mount,*
> *HAMBLEDON,*
> *HB13 7TY*

or

> *Mrs J Carter*
> *16 Abbey Mount*
> *HAMBLEDON*
> *HB13 7TY*

Many people prefer the indented style for handwritten addresses and the blocked style for typed or printed addresses, but there is no necessary convention to follow. However, if you have used a blocked layout for your letter, it is probably better to use a blocked layout for the envelope as well, especially for formal or business letters.

County names are no longer required in UK postal addresses, since the postal town name and postcode provide sufficient information for delivery. There is no need to clutter the envelope with unnecessary information. However, if you prefer to include the county name, as some people still do, it should be on the line above the postcode. The postcode should always be on the bottom line of an address.

Postcodes should be written in capitals on a separate line. There is no punctuation in a postcode, but leave a clear space (two character spaces if you are typing the address) between the two parts.

Punctuation

- No punctuation is required in addresses, and postal services generally prefer there not to be any. Nevertheless, many people still like to add commas at the end of every line (except the last) when using the indented style of layout and/or when handwriting the address.

- There should be no comma between a house number and the street name.

- If the address includes a house name, do not put inverted commas round the name.

- There should be no underlining in an address.

- Country abbreviations should not include full stops: *UK, USA*.

- Other abbreviations generally (but not always) follow the usual conventions for including or omitting full stops (see page 167): *Yorks, W Lothian*. As a general rule, do not use full stops in the blocked style (which always has minimal or no punctuation); with the indented style, some full stops are acceptable.

Addresses abroad

Not surprisingly, the conventions for addressing envelopes differ from country to country, and it would be impossible to cover all such conventions in this book.

In general, the safest way of handling foreign addresses is to copy carefully any address you have been given, especially with regard to layout and spelling. Even if you do not speak the language of the country concerned, it should be fairly obvious which part is a building number and street name, which part is a town or city, and which part if any is a postal code. Separating these out in accordance with UK postal practice may not quite correspond to the conventions of the receiving country, but its postal service will probably be able to understand what is intended. Note the following points:

- It is always best to write or print at least the town or city name in capital letters. By convention this is expected in many countries, and even where it is not expected, it is good practice to do so.

- It is even better practice to write or print the entire address in capital letters, as this is expected or recommended in some countries, such as the USA (see below) and Canada.

- The words for 'street', 'road', etc are not written with initial capital letters in some languages: e.g. in France, *rue d'Ankara* (*rue* = 'Road').

- In many countries, the house or building number follows the street name:

> *GANSSTRASSE 27*
> *4051 BASEL*
> *SWITZERLAND*

- Postal codes in other countries are not always placed on a separate line as they are in the UK. For example, in France the postcode is written on the same line as the name of the town or city and precedes it:

5 RUE D'ANKARA
67009 STRASBOURG

In Canada, the town name, province and postcode are all written on the same line:

ORLEANS ONTARIO K1C 1W2

The province is generally indicated by its two-letter code:

ORLEANS ON K1C 1W2

Australian addresses have a similar format, with the state or territory abbreviation and the postcode written on the same line as the town name:

LAKEWOOD NSW 2443

NOTE: A list of the standard postal abbreviations for American states, Canadian provinces and territories, and Australian states and territories can be found on pages 169–72.

- Do not punctuate foreign addresses, as the postal services of many countries (such as the USA and Canada) prefer no punctuation (except apostrophes that are part of proper names, such as *St John's*).

- Accents and diacritics on letters and hyphens between words should generally be retained (but note, for example, that the French postal authorities recommend that town and city names should be printed in capital letters without accents, therefore *Orléans* would be written *ORLEANS*). If you do omit hyphens, replace them with single spaces.

Addressing mail to the USA

As was mentioned above, addresses on mail to the USA should be entirely in capital letters and without punctuation marks. The officially recommended layout is:

First line: ADDRESSEE'S NAME
Second line: NUMBER, STREET, APARTMENT NUMBER or
                   POST OFFICE BOX NUMBER
Third line: CITY, STATE, ZIP CODE (= US postcode)
Fourth line: UNITED STATES OF AMERICA

Postal information available online

There is a great deal of postal and addressing information now available on the internet: try googling 'postal addresses', 'postal codes', 'post codes', 'postal information', etc, plus the name of the country you need information about. Most countries (possibly all countries) have an official post office website where you may find information on postal address conventions.

At present, over a hundred countries of the Universal Postal Union (UPU) use postal codes as part of postal addresses. Information about these countries' codes can be found on the UPU website (www.upu.int). This site also has links to the websites of the postal administrations of UPU member countries, where more information on address styles and conventions can often be found. Many of these sites, though not all of them, have information in English.

Return addresses

It is wise to put a return address on all important letters, and quite sensible to do so on any letter you send. The return address should be written on the back of the envelope, in such a way as to make it clear that it *is* the return address (for example, written in smaller letters than you have used on the front of the envelope, at an angle or in a corner, or prefixed with 'Sender:' or 'From:' or 'If undelivered, return to:').

In Canada and the USA, the convention is to write the return address in the top left-hand corner of the front of the envelope, not on the back of the envelope. You may wish to follow this convention when writing to someone in North America, but note that it would clash with the correct positioning of an 'Airmail' label.

Stamps

Stamps should always be placed in the top right-hand corner of the envelope.

Airmail

If you are sending a letter by airmail, you should affix a blue 'Airmail' label to the envelope in the top left-hand corner. Alternatively, you can write or print 'Par Avion – By Airmail', or simply 'Airmail', in the top left-hand corner. You can, of course, also buy and send pre-printed airletters.

4 Email

The benefits of emailing . . .

For many people nowadays, email is steadily replacing both letters and telephone calls as a regular means of communication. Its benefits are clear: it's quicker than writing and posting a letter, and as a means of communicating with more than one person, it is more convenient than phoning – and, in addition, you have a record of what has been said.

There are, of course, some situations (such as expressions of sympathy or condolences) in which an email might be felt to lack the personal touch that a handwritten letter would have, and sometimes thanks or apologies might be more appropriately expressed in a letter (though in other circumstances an email would be quite acceptable). Equally, in some formal or business contexts an email would not yet be considered appropriate, though this is constantly changing as more and more people use and accept email as a normal means of written communication. It depends on the circumstances and on your relationship with the person you are writing to, and only you can decide whether an email would be acceptable or whether a letter would be more suitable.

Of course, if a quick communication is needed, email has the benefit of immediacy, but you may need to apologise for emailing rather than writing. Similarly, if you only have someone's email address and not

If in doubt, err on the safe side and be conventional: **a letter will not offend, but an email might.**

their postal address, you will have to email even if you know a letter would be more appropriate, in which case you should apologise for your informality and put your postal address in the email so that the recipient can choose to reply by email or letter.

. . . and the dangers

The very ease with which emails can be written and sent has led to some problems and dangers you need to be aware of and avoid.

First, email can be a useful way of communicating privately or secretly with someone – but you don't know who will be looking over the recipient's shoulder when they open your email, so you had better label it 'Confidential'. And remember that your email may remain on file and be open to inspection. Offensive or libellous comments are no less offensive or libellous simply because they are made in emails.

Second, because writing and sending emails is so quick and easy, many people fire them off one after another without sufficient thought about their usefulness. Particularly bad are emails sent around simply 'for your information', copying people in without the sender giving serious thought as to whether the recipients will need, expect or value the information they are being sent. Most people have more than enough email to read as it is, so do not send information unless it is necessary; email only those who need to know.

And third, remember that one of the major benefits of emailing – its very speed and immediacy – is also one of its major drawbacks. Once the 'Send' button is pressed, an email is on its way and is almost impossible to retrieve. (Some email systems do provide a 'Recall email' facility, but you've got to be pretty quick at recalling or it's too late.) Always make sure – doubly sure! – before you send an email not only that it says what you want it to say but that you are sending it *only* to the person/people you intend it for. Keep away from the 'Send' button until you have checked who is in the address box. And take particular care with the 'Reply' button – who exactly is going to receive a copy of your reply?

The external structure of an email

The 'From' heading and your username

The first line of an email states your identity as the sender, using your username. You can choose whatever username you like, but ideally it should be similar to your own name so that you are easily identifiable. If you have chosen a rather odd or amusing username for emails to friends and family, you might perhaps think of using a more serious one for formal and business emails.

The address box: 'To: . . .'

The recipient's address must, of course, be typed correctly, but since most people now have a contacts file attached to their email account, this is not a great problem.

If there is more than one address in the 'To' box, they should be separated by commas or semicolons. This is generally done automatically if you lift addresses from your contacts file.

CC and BCC: who gets copied in?

The 'CC' box is where you key the email address of anyone to whom you want to send a copy of an email. (CC means 'carbon copy', a term that dates back to the days when typists used sheets of carbon paper to make copies of documents they were typing.) In general, people listed in the CC box are only being kept informed; they are not expected to act on the contents of the email. If you expect action from them, put them in the 'To' box.

> If it is likely that the recipient(s) of the email will not recognise the people in the CC box from their email addresses, it would be polite to tell them in the email itself who else you are copying in: e.g. 'I am copying this email to . . .'

Addresses listed in the CC box will be visible to all recipients of the email. If you want to copy an email to someone without other people's knowledge or without revealing their email address, you must enter them in the 'BCC' box. The use of BCC (which means 'blind carbon copy') is sometimes looked on with disapproval, as it seems a little underhanded to send copies of emails to people without the main recipient(s) knowing you have done so. But there may be issues of privacy involved, for example when you have been given someone's email address in confidence and must not reveal it to anyone else.

> In business, using BCC is one way of communicating information to a number of clients without revealing who your clients are.

The subject line

The subject line gives a brief indication of the subject matter of your email. When emailing friends, you may write amusing or cryptic subject lines, but in formal and business emails you must endeavour to create a subject line that clearly states what the email is about. An email with a cryptic or supposedly amusing subject line may well be taken for spam and deleted unread. There are a number of points to bear in mind:

- A subject line must be brief, otherwise the end of it may be lost. Put the most informative words at the beginning, so that if the end of the line does not appear, the purpose of the email will still be fairly clear. For example, 'Looking for information about the recent tes' is not a very helpful subject line, whereas 'CO2 emission test results: where can I fin', although equally incomplete, gives a clear idea of the point of the email.

- In formal and business emails, the subject line should contain all the details that might be needed to identify the email and its contents at a later date. For example, 'Finance committee; minutes of meeting 12/10/09' is more helpful than 'Yesterday's meeting'.

- Do not write the subject line in capital letters. And do not use abbreviations unless you are sure the recipient will understand what is meant; in general, spell words out in full.

- If you mark the email 'Confidential' in the subject line, do not put anything in the subject line that might indicate what the confidential matter is.

Re:

Do not write 'Re:' at the start of the subject line. This is only found in email replies. Since senders of spam often use 'Re:' to try to persuade people that the spam is in fact a reply to a previous email, if you use 'Re:' in your subject line, your email may well be taken for spam and deleted unopened.

Abbreviations used in subject lines

'Q:'   indicates that the email contains a question.
'Req:'   indicates a request.
'FYI:'   ('for your information') indicates that the email is only for the recipient's information, and no action is required.
'FAO:' ('for the attention of') can be used to specify a person within an organisation to whom the email is addressed.

The internal structure of an email

The salutation and the complimentary close

Most of the information about the salutation and the complimentary close in letters (see Chapter 1) applies to emails as well. How you open and close your email will, of course, depend on who you are writing to and for what purpose. Although some people consider it acceptable to omit the salutation in all but the most formal or business emails, there are others who are quite offended by emails that do not observe the basic conventions of letter-writing. In a formal or business email you should certainly include a proper salutation and complimentary close.

In informal and even fairly formal emails, some people consider it acceptable simply to start with the recipient's name without a preceding

'Dear' (or even 'Hi' or 'Hello'). Others, however, find this much too brusque, bordering on rude, so in most circumstances it may be safer to put in a full salutation, whether formal or informal.

As with the salutation, the complimentary close will vary from informal to formal/conventional, but you should always give at least your name at the end of the message. This also serves the purpose of showing that the full message has been received and that nothing has been lost in transmission.

In an email you generally do not put your address or the date at the beginning of the message. (The date is generated automatically and included in the heading of the email.) If you want to add your address, phone number or other details, put them below your name at the end of the email. Some authorities recommend that you include your email address, as some mailers strip out this information from the heading. If you are emailing your MP (or other political representative), you should always include your postal address, as they will want to know that you are, in fact, one of their constituents.

The body of the message

Most of what was said in Chapter 1 about the style and content of a letter applies equally to emails, and need not be repeated here. Your layout within the email – whether indented or blocked – should follow the recommendations for letters given above, though many people prefer a blocked layout for all emails, formal or informal.

Do not use the subject line as the opening line of your email. Repeat the subject within the text of the email. For example, if the subject of your email was 'Latest CO2 emission test results', you should not begin your email with 'I was looking at these this morning . . .', but rather 'I was looking at the latest CO2 emission test results this morning . . .'.

If you are adding one or more attachments, you should explain in the email what the attachments are.

And finally, since not all emails are informal, it is not always appropriate (and is often totally inappropriate) to use the sort of abbreviations commonly found in text messages, such as BTW ('by the way') or HTH ('hope this helps'). Write emails in normal everyday English.

5 Planning, writing and checking letters and emails

For a casual chatty letter or email to a friend or relative, you would normally just sit down and write without planning or checking, but a formal or business letter (such as a letter of complaint, a letter to your MP or a job application) will almost certainly require some thought and planning, and you would be wise not to send off such a letter without checking it over – more than once.

For 'difficult' letters, on the other hand, such as letters of condolence, the hardest thing is making a start at all, and it is therefore better in the first instance not to worry too much about what to say, but simply to get *something* written down which you can discard, change or add to as you work towards a final satisfactory version.

NOTE: For convenience, to avoid having to repeat 'letters or emails' time after time, we will from here on in this chapter refer only to letters, but everything should be understood to be equally valid for emails as well.

Planning your letter

When planning your letter, there are several questions you should ask yourself:

- **Why am I writing? What do I intend to achieve by means of my letter?**
  The aim of any letter is to communicate something to someone. To do so effectively, therefore, you must be quite clear about what you

are trying to communicate and what you are hoping to accomplish by doing so.

- **Am I writing to the right person?**
  Can the person you are writing to act on the information you are providing? Can they deal with your request or your complaint?

- **What information am I intending to convey? How much do I need to say?**
  Have you got all the necessary information? How much of this information are you going to include? How much can you assume the other person already knows? What do they need to know that they might not know already? And what do they obviously know and not need to be told by you? Will they require a lengthy detailed explanation or argument, or will a quick summary of the relevant points be sufficient? Only give as much information as necessary to make your point.

- **Does anyone else need to know?**
  Are you going to copy your letter to anyone other than the person you are writing to? Copying letters is a good way of keeping people informed, but it can be a perfect nuisance if overdone. Does anyone else *really* need a copy of what you have said?

- **What response do I want?**
  What response do you want from the recipient of the letter? Are you expecting information from them, or an apology, or just an acknowledgement of what you have written? Do you want them to do something, and if so, what – for instance, if you are complaining about faulty goods, do you want a replacement or your money back?

- **Is a letter the appropriate means of communication?**
  Might a phone call, for example, be better, or a face-to-face talk? Sometimes a letter can seem to be making a mountain out of a molehill. If a neighbour's cat is digging up your garden, for example, it is surely better to simply go round and speak to the cat's owner rather than writing a letter, which might make the problem more of an

issue than it need be. There are situations, however, when writing a letter is the right way to proceed.

- **What sort of letter should I write? Would an email be acceptable?**
  There are some situations (such as expressions of thanks, sympathy, apologies or condolences) in which the personal touch of a hand-written letter is more appropriate than a typed letter or an email. There are also, at the other end of the spectrum, some situations in which an email might not be considered formal enough – perhaps suggesting a lack of seriousness, commitment or courtesy – and where only a properly written or typed letter would do. If the latter is the case, does your letter need to conform to a particular format or layout, such as the blocked style (see page 11) which is best for a business letter? How formal or informal should the tone of your letter be?

Drafting and writing your letter

Once you have planned your letter in outline, you are ready to draft and/or write it. Your aim at this stage is to take the answers to the questions you have asked yourself at the planning stage and form them into a letter that matches your purpose and conveys your message. (This may sound a bit over the top, but implicitly it is what you do every time you write a letter.)

Online help

Word-processing packages often provide template letters. You may also find specimens for various types of letters on the internet. Make use of these if it helps, but do check whether these sites are oriented towards British or American usage. And do *adapt* the specimens for your specific purpose, don't just *adopt* them willy-nilly.

Think of the structure, presentation and content of your letter

A well-laid-out letter will make a good impression on your behalf right from the start, and is therefore more likely to be read with goodwill and attention. This is particularly important for formal and business letters.

- From your planning, estimate how many sheets of paper you are likely to need and therefore what size of paper to use (if you have a choice; see page 19).

- Are you going to use a blocked or indented layout (see Chapter 1)?

- Does your letter need a subject line or heading that will immediately tell the recipient what the letter is about? (A business letter usually will; a more informal letter usually won't.)

- How are you going to give your letter a clear, coherent and logical structure, so that the reader can easily follow your information or argument? How are going to divide up your letter into paragraphs? (A paragraph is usually built round one main point. When you move on to the next point, start a new paragraph.) What will be the most effective order in which to make the various points you want to make?

Write your letter

- Begin your letter with a brief introductory paragraph outlining what you are writing about. In a business letter, you may want to refer to a telephone call or conversation you have had or to previous correspondence.

- Follow this introductory paragraph with one or more paragraphs setting out the point(s) you want to make in a logical sequence, providing relevant details where required. (Would it be easier to read if you presented some of your information in the form of bullet points or data tables?)

Beware of bees in bonnets and axes to grind

If writing about something you feel strongly about, be careful to keep a sense of proportion.

- Make sure there is clear, objective justification for what you say.

- Do not say 'Everybody knows . . .' – in most cases, everybody does *not* know.

- Beware of repeating conspiracy theories – most of them are nonsense.

- Do not write your letter in capital letters or punctuate it with exclamation marks.

- Do not write or sign your letter in green ink.

Politeness is all

If you want results, be polite. Remember: 'There's no excuse for abuse'.

- Do not write anything that you wouldn't say to someone face to face.

- Do not write anything that would hurt the other person's feelings.

- Do not question your correspondent's sanity, morals or parentage.

- Do not impute motives you cannot possibly be sure of.

- Do not assume the truth of what you cannot possibly know for certain.

- Close with a short final paragraph thanking the person for their help, asking for a response, etc.

- Keep paragraphs short. This makes the information easier to follow.

- Make your point(s) briefly and succinctly. Don't ramble or wander off the point. Avoid long-windedness, but do not be so brief as to appear rude.

- Do not say 'we' when you mean 'I'.

- When typing formal letters, don't get carried away with the huge variety of font and colour options available to you. Keep to one simple font, in black.

Keep it simple

Do not imagine that you will improve the tone or impact of your letter by using 'big' words unnecessarily. Whatever can be said, can and should be said in simple English. If you try to impress the person you are writing to by using long words, you may fail to get your message across effectively. You do not need to use high-flown language to write formal or business letters: 'formal' does not mean 'pompous'.

Of course, you may need to use technical terminology. That is entirely different. But only use technical terms as an aid to communication, not to parade your specialist knowledge; and always put yourself in the position of your reader – will they understand what you have said, or do you need to explain the technical words you have used? In particular, beware of abbreviations and jargon that you may be familiar with but your correspondent may not.

'Topping and tailing' your letter

There are certain style conventions with regard to the salutations (see page 7) and complimentary closes (see page 8) of informal and formal letters. Informal letters are often closed with 'Yours sincerely'. (More informally, you could end your letter simply with 'Yours', 'Best wishes' or 'Kind regards'; and of course to family or friends you could write something like 'With love', 'Much love', 'With lots of love', 'Best wishes', 'Love and best wishes', 'All the best', or simply 'Love'.)

In formal letters to someone whose name you know, you address the person by name in the salutation: e.g. 'Dear Dr Brown'. In this case, you use 'Yours sincerely' in the complimentary close. If you do not know the name of the person you are writing to, you begin with 'Dear Sir', 'Dear Sirs', 'Dear Sir or Madam', etc, and close with 'Yours faithfully'.

Do not use phrases like 'Yours very sincerely' or 'Yours respectfully'. They sound rather old-fashioned and, even worse, insincere or affectedly humble. 'Yours truly' is also a bit old-fashioned now. Keep to 'Yours sincerely' and 'Yours faithfully'.

Checking your letter

When you have written your letter, you need to check it over. You will need to read it at least twice, perhaps even three times for a very important letter. You are now looking out for the following things:

- **content**
- **grammar**, **vocabulary** and **style**
- **spelling** and **punctuation**

Content

When your letter is being read by the person you are writing to, you will not be present to correct any misunderstandings, so your letter must provide all the necessary information set out in such a way that the reader understands what you mean.

- Does your letter say what it should? Does it say everything you want to say, but no more than you need to say? (It is very easy to get carried away.) Look for passages that are irrelevant or repetitious, and delete them.

- Will the reader be able to home in on the key points? Is it clear why you are writing and what you are expecting by way of a response? Have you ordered your paragraphs logically?

- If you think you have been particularly clever at some point, triumphantly delivering an especially smart or telling blow, be very careful. Will what you have said with such satisfaction today make you cringe with embarrassment tomorrow – after you have sent the letter off?

Checking tips

- If possible, take a break between writing your letter and checking it over. Coming back to it fresh may help you spot things you did not see before.

- If you have been working onscreen, print out your letter before editing it. You are more likely to spot errors reading your letter on paper than reading it onscreen. This is true also for emails – print and check before sending.

- A good way of checking what you have written is to read it out loud to yourself.

- If it is a particularly important letter, get someone else to read it over. They may spot errors you have missed or see that parts of your letter are not as clear as you thought they were.

Grammar, vocabulary and style

Having checked the content of your letter, you need to check how well you have expressed yourself, by looking at your grammar and the words you have used.

- Consult Quick Reference 3, page 184. Check you are not making any of the common errors of grammar and vocabulary listed there.

- Check for slang and unsuitable colloquialisms in formal letters. Apply the 'newsreader' and 'Queen' tests to any questionable term: ask yourself whether you could imagine a newsreader saying it on television, or the Queen saying it in a speech? If the answer is 'no', it is not suitable for a formal letter.

- Look out for clichés and overused phrases. When all is said and done, at the end of the day, and taking one thing with another, they will not add much to your letter (just as the first three phrases add nothing to the sense of this sentence). They are usually unnecessary clutter, and often a mask for lazy and unclear thinking.

- Be sensitive to cultural and linguistic differences. Have you written anything that the recipient of your letter might not understand? For the same reason, be careful with jokes: other people may not share your sense of humour.

- Be very cautious if using online grammar and style checkers. They may give you bad advice. Also make sure that they are not giving you advice based on American rather than British English.

I have to say that I am writing to complain . . .

Some experts are of the opinion that you should never begin a letter or email with 'I am writing to say/complain/inquire . . .' because it is obvious that you are writing. However, it seems a harmless and often useful opener to your first paragraph and there is no reason to avoid it.

On the other hand, avoid beginning sentences with 'I have to say . . .' (e.g. 'I have to say I was surprised to receive your letter'). If you have to say it, just say it: 'I was surprised to receive your letter.'

Spelling and punctuation

The last stage of checking is for spelling and punctuation. As with grammar and vocabulary, you should consult Quick Reference 3, page 184.

When checking your spelling, do not rely solely on a computer spellchecker, as it is not foolproof. It will pick up typing errors (e.g. *godo* for *good*) but will not alert you to a correctly spelt word used in the wrong context (e.g. *coarse* instead of *course*).

Writing emails

As far as drafting, writing and checking are concerned, email-writing is essentially the same as letter-writing, and what was said in the previous sections of this chapter applies equally here. Writing emails requires just as much care and mental effort as writing letters. Emailing is no excuse for carelessness, casualness or sloppy thought and writing.

There are, however, some specific points to be made with regard to emails that do not apply to letters:

- Because of software differences, what looks fine on your computer may come out as garbage on another person's. For example, some formatting options such as the 'Tab' facility and bullet points do not always transfer well. For bullet points, choose another option, such as asterisks. To preserve other formatting, it may be better to send the document as an attachment rather than in the body of an email.

- For highlighting and emphasis, write the text between underscores (_xx_), asterisks (*xx*) or angle brackets (>xx<), or in capital letters (XX). Some people dislike the use of capitals, as it looks like 'shouting' (see the section on 'Netiquette' below), but it is acceptable for a word or two. Titles may be keyed in italics or between quotation marks, angle brackets or underscores.

- Special characters can cause problems, and you may have to add a note to your email explaining that such and such a character will appear as '&x;' on the receiving computer. Accents and diacritics on letters can also cause problems, and may have to be written after the letter they are attached to. Write subscript numbers in the form CO_2, and superscripts as x^2.

- Emoticons and smileys should not be used in formal emails, though smileys can be useful in less formal emails to indicate that something is not to be taken seriously or at face value.

- Only use text-message abbreviations in very informal emails to friends who you know will understand them.

Replies

- Before clicking on the 'Reply' icon, check the address line – make sure you are only replying to the individual(s) you intend to contact. If your mailer has a 'Reply All' button, do not click on this unless you really do want to reply to 'All'.

- If you are copying any new recipient (s) into your reply, bear in mind that they will also see the original message (unless you delete it).

- In a long correspondence, when replies build up into increasingly long emails, it is sensible to cut out any unwanted material from previous emails, and leave only the portion of the text you are replying to.

Netiquette

Over the years, various conventions for internet etiquette, or 'netiquette', have evolved. It is important to be aware of these, and to respect them. Some of them, such as the content of the subject line, have been covered above in Chapter 4. Here are some others:

- Do not write in capital letters. This is known as 'shouting'. (Capitals may, however, be used to emphasise short passages in emails, though there are alternative ways of doing this which many people prefer – see the second bullet point of the 'Writing emails' section above.)

- Write in correct English; spell and punctuate carefully. Check what you have written.

- If cross-posting (that is, sending the same material to more than one group of recipients), apologise for doing so, as some people may get more than one copy of your email, and this can be irritating.

- If you are forwarding an email to someone else, add a note saying where the original message came from and why you are forwarding it. If you add anything, make it clear which part of the forwarded message is yours. If you cut out parts of the original message, show clearly where you have made deletions.

- Large attachments can fill up people's email inboxes, so it is always wise to check with an intended recipient whether or not they are willing and able to receive the attachment you want to send. One authority recommends that you send nothing over 100 kilobytes without permission, though others do not place the limit quite as low as this. If possible, reduce the attachment in size before sending it, using one of the available software packages. And when sending an email attachment, state clearly in the email what the attachment contains.

- With large quantities of information available on websites, and search engines that can trawl these websites for that information, it is increasingly easy nowadays to find the answer to almost any question on the internet. However, if you want to follow up something you have found (or perhaps not found) online, by emailing an expert with a question, it is polite to first check whether they are willing to receive emailed questions. Introduce yourself and explain your reason for contacting them. Say where you found their email address. And do not ask for or expect a reply by return – people have other things to do, and answering your crucial query is not necessarily a priority in their lives.

- Never fire off an email in anger. Stop, think, take a deep breath, go for a walk – do anything but reply by return. That is the trouble with email – it is too easy to send off a quick reply, which you may then regret but be unable to retrieve. Sending angry, abusive emails is known as 'flaming'. Don't send flame mail (and if you receive any, don't respond to it). Cyberbullying is still bullying. And if you put obscenities in your emails, some mailers will not deliver them (which is probably a good thing).

- Do not forget 'Please' and 'Thank you'. (Some people have the odd idea that emailing does not require the common courtesies.) And always write your name at the end.

Email and the law

Remember that, even in electronic form, an email is a document. In many countries nowadays, emails are considered legal documents acceptable in court, and email is subject to the same laws as those covering other forms of written communication. Agreements made by email will be legally binding, and emails and their attachments are subject, for example, to both copyright law and libel law.

Email is not a vehicle for confidential communication. Write nothing that you would not want to be made public – because it might be.

6 Invitations and replies

Invitations to events such as parties, dinners, weddings or bar mitzvahs can range across the spectrum from the very formal to the totally off-beat, but whatever style of invitation you choose, to whatever sort of event you are holding, an invitation must include:

- who is being invited;
- who they are being invited by;
- what they are being invited to;
- where and when the event will take place.

Make clear, either in the invitation or in an accompanying note, whether the invitation includes a couple's children or only the couple themselves, and whether a single invitee may bring a partner.

It is helpful to include in or along with an invitation:

- an address to reply to, and the date by which a reply should be received;
- any special dress requirements on the day (see page 57).

Invitations should be sent out well in advance, so that the invitees have enough notice of the event and time to reply, and you have time to make the arrangements to cater for all those who say they are coming. For example, at least two or three months' notice would be expected for a formal gathering such as a wedding.

'Save the Day' cards

If you want to give your family and friends advance notice of an important event, before you are ready to send out proper invitations, you could use 'Save the Day' (or 'Save the Date') cards. These are 'pre-invitation' announcements of a forthcoming event, asking the recipients to keep that day free. You should add that they will receive a proper invitation at a later date.

You don't need much information on a Save the Day card; something along the following lines is enough:

Save the Date!
Tony & Sandra are getting married
on 24 November 2010,
and hope you will be there
to celebrate with them.
Invitations will be sent out
early next year.

Or even shorter:

Please save the date!
Our wedding will be on
Wednesday 24 November 2010
Tony & Sandra

Of course, you will probably want to make your card a little fancier than this. Discuss it with a printer or stationer, or go online to see what sort of cards are available (or even just to get ideas for cards you can make yourself). How about a 'Save the Day' fridge magnet, so that people are constantly reminded of the date?

Formal invitations

A formal invitation, such as a wedding invitation, can be in the form of a printed card or a handwritten or typed letter. (It can also be printed from a computer, so long as the printer will support a suitable paper format and attractive typefaces.)

Printed cards

- Formal invitations are usually printed on white card, but other pale colours such as cream or ivory are also suitable, especially for invitations to weddings or wedding anniversaries. The card can be flat and printed on one side only, or folded (like most greetings cards) with 'Wedding Invitation' (or whatever is appropriate for the occasion) on the front and the text of the invitation printed on the right-hand inside page. Keep the decoration simple, such as a fine gold or silver line round the card and/or a deckle or scalloped edge.

- The cards are usually printed in black ink, but other colours are acceptable, again especially for wedding or anniversary invitations, which might have gold or silver lettering (but make sure that the printing is easily readable on whatever colour of card you have chosen).

- The lettering for formal invitations is a matter of choice, but whatever typeface you choose, make sure that it is not too florid. The text needs to be readable, especially names, addresses and postcodes.

- Formal invitations on cards do not include a date, a salutation ('Dear Jim') or a complimentary close ('Yours sincerely' or 'Love from . . .').

- Formal invitations on printed cards are always written in the third person (that is, 'Mr and Mrs Joseph Smith request the pleasure of the company of . . .' rather than 'We request . . .' or 'You are invited . . .').

- The invitation may be a general one without any specified names (that is, 'Mr and Mrs Joseph Smith request the pleasure of your company . . .') or they may be personalised with the name(s) of the individual invitee(s) (that is, 'Mr and Mrs Joseph Smith request the pleasure of the company of Dr and Mrs Peter Foster . . .').

- If you are using the impersonal formula 'your company', write the invitees' names in the top right-hand corner of the cards to make it clear who is being invited.

- If you are putting the names of your guests into the text of the invitation, it is normal to have the invitation printed with a blank line. For example, for a wedding invitation:

Mr and Mrs Joseph Smith
request the pleasure of the company of

_____

at the wedding of their daughter Susan
to . . . . . .

You then write in the names by hand (the names can be printed if you prefer, but writing them by hand gives the invitations a more personal touch). To match the quality of the printed card, you should write in ink, not ballpoint pen, or you could use a calligraphy pen to add that special touch.

- Instead of 'request the pleasure of your company', you could say 'request the honour of your presence'. While perhaps rather too formal and deferential for family and friends, it might be appropriate for high-ranking guests.

- Titles and ranks, whether of the bride, the groom, the hosts or the guests, should always be included on formal invitations. (For correct forms for titles and ranks, see Quick Reference 2, page 173.)

- How to address or refer to children in a formal invitation can be problematic. Young children should be included in their parents' invitations, and addressed by their names only (without titles). Older children and young adults should get their own invitations and be addressed as adults. At what age this change should take place is a matter of personal choice; the age of 15 is sometimes suggested as a suitable point, but nowadays a younger teenager may well expect to be treated as an adult.

• The letters RSVP may be added, generally at the bottom left-hand corner of the card, with an address to which replies should be sent and, if you wish, a date by which replies should be received. (RSVP is an abbreviation of the French phrase *Répondez s'il vous plaît*, which means 'Please reply'.)

If after a wedding there is to be a celebration meal, then this too should be mentioned in the invitation. A full formal wedding invitation on a card could, therefore, look something like this:

Mr and Mrs Joseph Smith
request the pleasure of the company of

Dr and Mrs Peter Foster, Gemma Foster and Guy Foster

at the wedding of their daughter Susan
to Mr Graham Knowles
at St Martin's Church, Grout Street, Stambourne,
on Saturday 10th July at 3pm,
and afterwards
at the Goose Inn, Stambourne

RSVP by 30th April
73 Roseberry Place, Stambourne, MQ4 6TX

If you want to indicate that the invitee may bring a partner, whose name you may not know, the invitation can be addressed to, for example, 'Mr Michael Brown and guest' or 'Miss Eileen O'Neill and partner'.

It is normal not to close an invitation with a full stop. Commas are useful, but keep them to a minimum, as in the examples printed here.

Variations on wedding invitations

If the bride's parents are no longer married, and the bride's mother has not remarried, the first lines of the card should read:

> *Mr Joseph Smith and Mrs Joseph Smith*
> *request the pleasure of the company of* . . . . . .

If the former Mrs Joseph Smith has remarried, the card should read:

> *Mr Joseph Smith and Mrs Henry Irving*
> *request the pleasure of the company of* . . . . . .

If the mother and stepfather of the bride are hosting the wedding, the style is:

> *Mr and Mrs Henry Irving*
> *request the pleasure of the company of*
>
> _____
>
> *at the wedding of her daughter Susan*
> *to* . . . . . .
> *at* . . . . . .

Note that the invitation should refer to 'her' daughter, not 'their' daughter.

If divorced and remarried parents are jointly hosting the wedding, a possible wording on the card would be the following:

> *Mr and Mrs Joseph Smith*
> *and*
> *Mr and Mrs Henry Irving*
> *request the pleasure of the company of*
>
> _____
>
> *at the wedding of Susan Smith*
> *to* . . . . . .

This avoids any need to refer to 'his/her/their' daughter.

Of course, in many marriages, the bride and groom may be acting as their own hosts. The style for invitations in such circumstances is:

> *Mr Samuel Kellett and Miss Sara Onoro*
> *request the pleasure of the company of*
>
> _____
>
> *at their wedding*
> *at St Martin's Church . . . . . .*
> *on . . . . . .*

Church blessing

In yet another variant, the marriage ceremony itself may be a small affair at a registry office, followed by a church blessing to which guests are invited. The invitations will therefore read:

> *Mr Samuel Kellett and Miss Sara Onoro*
> *request the pleasure of the company of*
>
> _____
>
> *at a blessing of their marriage*
> *at . . . . . .*

Civil partnerships

For a civil partnership ceremony or 'ceremony of commitment', the invitation might read:

> *Miss Sarah Adams and Miss Vicki Green*
> *request the pleasure of your company*
> *at the celebration of their civil partnership*
> *at . . . . . .*

Evening invitations

It is not always possible to invite as many guests as one might like to a wedding. For this reason, many couples now invite a wider circle of friends to an 'evening reception' after the main wedding meal. An invitation of this sort might read:

Mr and Mrs Joseph Smith
request the pleasure of the company of

_____

at an evening reception
to celebrate the marriage of their daughter Susan
to Mr Graham Knowles,
at the Goose Inn, Stambourne,
on Saturday 10th July at 8pm

Other celebrations

The above sections have concentrated on weddings and similar ceremonies, but the general style of invitations to any formal occasion is essentially the same. Here are two examples:

Mr and Mrs Lionel Fischer
request the pleasure of your company
at a dinner
to celebrate the Bar Mitzvah
of their son Richard
at the Goose Inn, Stambourne,
on Saturday 10th July at 7.30pm

Mr and Mrs Joseph Smith
request the pleasure of the company of

_____

at a luncheon
to celebrate their golden wedding
at the Goose Inn, Stambourne,
on Saturday 10th July at 12.30pm

Wedding anniversaries

It is not strictly correct to speak of a 'silver/ruby/golden/diamond wedding anniversary'; a 25th wedding anniversary is a 'silver wedding', a 50th wedding anniversary is a 'golden wedding', and so on.

Formal letters

Formal invitations of the type outlined above need not be sent out on cards. They can equally well be printed or written on notepaper, with the same layout and wording as above. Many people, however, prefer to send out invitations more in the form of a letter. The content of the letter should be in the same formal style as that described above for cards, but the address of the sender should be in the top right-hand corner of the letter, and it can be dated. There should not, however, be a salutation ('Dear . . .') or a complimentary close ('Yours sincerely').

Reply cards

If you want to be sure of a reply (and it is amazing how many people today do not have the simple courtesy to reply to an invitation, or to do so promptly), then you may like to include a reply card with your invitation. Again taking a wedding invitation as an example, a reply card would look something like this:

_____

would like to thank Mr and Mrs Joseph Smith
for their kind invitation
to the wedding of their daughter Susan
and to the reception afterwards
and will/but will not be able to attend

Notice that the use of the words 'would' and 'will' neatly and grammatically allows for one or more than one invitee. Another wording for the card could be:

will/will not be able to accept
the kind invitation of Mr and Mrs Joseph Smith
to the wedding of their daughter Susan

Alternatively, you might simply enclose a stamped, self-addressed envelope for replies, but leave it to the invitees to find a suitable card or sheet of paper to write on.

Additional information or questions

Do not clutter your invitation with unnecessary details (such as nearby hotels or where to park cars). Those can come later. Nevertheless, it can be helpful to give guests some idea of what is intended – for example, how they should dress, what and when they will be eating, and when an event is expected to begin and end – and there are some traditional words and phrases often used on invitations to convey this information succinctly.

Dress code (from the most to the least formal)

White tie: very formal evening dress for men, including a tailcoat and a white bow tie.

Morning dress: men's formal dress for daytime events; traditionally including a black tailcoat, silver tie and striped trousers, but many colour variations are now acceptable.

Black tie: men's formal evening wear including a dinner jacket and bow tie; although 'black tie' is specified, other colours of bow tie may be acceptable.

Informal: lounge suits for men.

Casual: could be anything; best to check if you see this on an invitation; some invitations specify 'smart casual', which would imply jackets, pullovers, and smart shirts as opposed to, for example, sandals, shorts and T-shirts.

Food (from the least to the most formal)

Cocktails: drinks accompanied with nuts, crisps and similar food to nibble.

Drinks and canapés: drinks and light snacks eaten before a main meal, e.g. after a wedding.

Buffet: something more substantial than light snacks, eaten while standing rather than at tables. (A 'finger buffet' consists of sandwiches, vol-au-vents, small pizza wedges, cocktail sausages, etc, which can be eaten with the fingers.)

Fork supper: more substantial than a buffet; food that can (supposedly) be eaten with a fork alone, e.g. pasta or rice dishes, seafood.

Supper party: an informal sit-down meal.

Dinner party: a formal dinner of several courses.

Time

7 for 7.30: guests should arrive between these two times, perhaps for a drink, before the main event starts at 7.30.

Carriages at 1 a.m.: the reception ends at 1 o'clock.

Till late: the event will continue to an unspecified late hour.

Less formal invitations

If you would prefer a slightly more informal approach, you may send out letters of invitation, in a normal letter style and format (see

Chapter 1) on appropriate paper and using a suitable quality of pen (see Chapter 2).

NOTE: In the examples that follow, addresses and dates will be omitted for space reasons.

In this informal approach, you simply write as you would speak (but don't forget to give all the essential information!). For example:

> Dear Uncle Peter and Aunt Joan,
>
> Simon and I are getting married on Saturday 11th September, and we do hope you and Sophie and Elaine will be able to come.
>
> The ceremony will be held at our local Methodist church (we'll send out maps to everyone who's coming so that no one gets lost) at 3 o'clock, and afterwards there will be a reception at the local pub, which really does excellent food (I was at a friend's 21st birthday party there last week).
>
> Please let us know if you will be able to join us for our special day. I do hope you can.
>
> Love to you all,
> Trish

Note that you don't need 'RSVP' because you have asked for a reply in the last paragraph of your letter.

An informal invitation to a ruby wedding might read as follows:

> My dear Nancy,
>
> Tom and I are having a small dinner party with a few close friends and family to celebrate our Ruby Wedding, and we hope that you and George will be able to join us to celebrate our forty years of 'wedded bliss'.
>
> The party will be at the local hotel, the one just along the street where we had that delightful meal last year when you were here with us. The dinner will be on the 21st (of course!), at 8pm,

and we are hoping that guests will join us at the hotel for champagne and some (short!) speeches at about 7.

I do hope you will be there to share happy memories with us. Please let us know if you will be able to come.

Our love and best wishes to you both,
Evelyn

Informal invitations of this sort could be made more interesting and personal by having suitable pictures or photographs copied on to them.

Reply cards

You can if you wish enclose a reply card with an informal invitation, but the wording should be simpler than for those accompanying formal invitations; for example:

---

will be delighted to join you
to celebrate your forty years of happy marriage

Emailed invitations

Email is of course useful if you want to send out informal invitations quickly to a large number of people. It is not really suitable for formal invitations, though, which should be on card or paper.

Replying to invitations

Reply to an invitation in the same style as the invitation itself. In other words, if you receive a formal invitation on a card, you should reply in an equally formal style, on a card or notepaper. Do not just reply by phone or face to face – if you have received a written or printed invitation, send a written reply.

Whatever you do, **do not forget to reply** and **do reply promptly.**

Try to give a clear 'yes' or 'no' if at all possible. If hosts need to make firm bookings for a meal, for example, they need to know in good time whether you will or will not be present. But see page 66 for how to deal with this.

Pre-printed reply cards

You can buy ready-made 'acceptance' and 'with regret' cards. Look in a stationer's or search online. The cards may be blank inside, in which case you will have to write your own acceptance/refusal, or they may be pre-printed along the following lines:

----

would like to thank

----

for their kind invitation,
and will have great pleasure in accepting

or:

----

will be pleased to accept
your kind invitation
to the marriage of

----

or for a refusal:

---

*will not be able to accept
the kind invitation of*

---

to the marriage of

---

and for a 21st birthday celebration:

---

*will not be able to accept
your kind invitation to dinner
to celebrate the 21st birthday of*

Reason for refusal

If you are sending back a refusal card, it is not necessary to state any reason for your refusal on the card (though some people prefer to add some catch-all phrase such as 'due to a previous engagement'), but it would be polite to include a separate note explaining why you are turning the invitation down.

Correspondence cards

Correspondence cards are (more or less) postcard-sized cards on which your personal details have been printed at the top:

*MR AND MRS THOMAS ADAIR
14 WELLS CLOSE BORTHWICH LINCS LT7 9TG
TEL: 03344 678 900*

Cards of this sort are ideal for writing formal or informal replies to invitations.

Formal acceptances and refusals

A formal acceptance, on a card or paper, is written in the same impersonal style as a formal invitation:

> *Dr and Mrs Peter Foster, Gemma Foster and Guy Foster thank Mr and Mrs Joseph Smith for their kind invitation to the wedding of their daughter Susan to Mr Graham Knowles at St Martin's Church, Grout Street, Stambourne, on Saturday 10th July at 3pm, and have great pleasure in accepting.*

or:

> *Dr and Mrs Peter Foster, Gemma Foster and Guy Foster thank Mr and Mrs Joseph Smith for their kind invitation to the wedding of their daughter Susan to Mr Graham Knowles at St Martin's Church, Grout Street, Stambourne, on Saturday 10th July at 3pm, but regret that they will be unable to attend.*

It is normal practice to repeat all the details given in the invitation, though it is not necessary to lay out your reply in an artistic style. When you write a formal reply like this, you do not sign it or make any other comment on it. If there is anything else you want to say, write it as a separate note; with a refusal, it would be polite to include a note explaining why you have to turn down the invitation.

Shorter versions without all the details are also acceptable:

> *Dr and Mrs Peter Foster, Gemma Foster and Guy Foster thank Mr and Mrs Joseph Smith for their kind invitation to their daughter's wedding, and to the reception afterwards, and have great pleasure in accepting.*

Reply even to refuse

Even if you are unable to attend the function you have been invited to, you *must* reply to the invitation, firstly to say thank you for being invited, and secondly to make it clear that you are not able to attend (as opposed to simply being too lazy to reply).

Replying on behalf of your partner

If you are replying on behalf of a partner as well as yourself, this style of reply would be acceptable:

> *Mr Michael Brown thanks Mr and Mrs Lionel Fischer for their kind invitation to himself and a partner to the celebration of the Bar Mitzvah of their son Richard, and has great pleasure in accepting.*

Stating the obvious for politeness' sake

If you have already agreed to be the best man, a bridesmaid or an usher at a wedding, everyone knows you will be there. Nevertheless, you should receive an official invitation, and you should reply to it. Not to do so would be extremely discourteous.

Informal acceptances and refusals

As with informal invitations, informal acceptances and refusals are written in the form of standard letters, with your address, a salutation, a complimentary close, etc. The text of a wedding acceptance letter to the bride's parents, if you don't know them very well (or not at all), could run along the following lines:

> *Dear Mr and Mrs Smith,*
>   *Peter and I would like to thank you for inviting us and Gemma and Guy to Susan and Graham's wedding next July, and we are delighted to accept.*

We have all been looking forward to the wedding so much since Susan sent us a 'save the day' card, and it has been marked up on our calendar in very big letters!

Apart from the pleasure of being with Susan and Graham on their special day, it will be nice to meet you and the rest of Susan's family at last. We often hear about you from Susan, so we feel we almost know you. You probably feel the same about us.

With thanks again for your kind invitation,

> *Yours sincerely,*
> *Helen Foster*

In an informal reply such as this, it is not necessary to repeat all the details from the invitation.

> If it is not clear whether or not children are included in the invitation, it is best to check on this before replying. Similarly, if you are single and the invitation names only you and not 'a partner', you are expected to come alone.

Of course, to a close friend an even more informal reply would be appropriate:

Dear Sara,

Thank you and Sam so much for inviting Nigel and me to your wedding in September. Of course we'll be delighted to come – we're looking forward to it already! Only the other day I was looking at some fabulous hats in Lewison's and wishing I had an excuse to buy one, and now I have! And I'll have to look for a posh frock as well.

I do hope the four of us will manage to get together before then, though. We've so much news to catch up on, and of course you'll be too busy on your wedding day to have any time for a

*proper chat. I'll give you a call next week and see if we can find a
night when we're all free. We might give that new Indian
restaurant a try; I've heard it's very good.*

Anyhow, we'll speak soon.

Love,
  Hannah

In a letter of refusal, it would be polite to explain why you are having
to turn down the invitation:

Dear Val,
  *Thanks for inviting us over for dinner a week on Saturday.
Unfortunately we already have an engagement for that evening,
as our next-door neighbours have invited us to their ruby
wedding celebrations. Isn't it just like the thing to get two
invitations for the same evening! Most weekends we are free.*
  *I hope we can get together soon, though. It's ages since we saw
each other. Sorry it doesn't work for that weekend, though.*

Love,
  Fran

Maybe yes, maybe no

If possible try to give a definite answer to an invitation right away. It
doesn't help the hosts' planning if they have a number of invitees who say
they may or may not be attending. However, if you hope to attend but there
are circumstances that prevent you from giving a definite 'yes', then say so:

• In reply to a **formal** invitation, you should send back a formal
  acceptance accompanied by a letter explaining that, while you are
  hoping to be able to attend, you are unable to give a definite commitment at this point. Explain the reason briefly, apologise for the
  inconvenience and assure the host that you will give them a firm
  decision as soon as you can.

- In reply to an **informal** invitation, you simply write a letter explaining that you hope to be able to come, but are unable to give a definite answer, again explaining why, apologising for the inconvenience and assuring the host of a definite answer as soon as possible.

Sending both a formal and an informal refusal

Many businesses today use PR companies to organise events for them. If you are invited to such an event, it is likely that you will receive a formal invitation. If you are unable to attend, all you need do is reply with a suitable formal refusal. Nevertheless, it is also a good idea to drop a less formal note to the person who really is behind the invitation, expressing regret and explaining why you cannot (or, if the event is past, could not) attend:

> *Mr Graham Thomson thanks Daimen Books for their kind invitation to celebrate their twenty-fifth anniversary at the Book Centre, Edinburgh, on Wednesday 26 May 2010, but regrets that he will be unable to attend.*

and then also:

> *Dear Ellen,*
>
> *I presume it was you who had my name added to the guest list for Daimen Books' 25th anniversary celebration next month. If so, thanks for thinking of me.*
>
> *I would love to be there to celebrate with you, but unfortunately I will be in Phuket at the time on a much-needed holiday. I won't be back in Edinburgh until the 30th.*
>
> *Anyhow, have a great time. I'll give you a call one day soon; perhaps we can do lunch or have a drink after work. It would be good to catch up.*
>
> *All the best for now,*
>
> *Graham*

7 Thank-you letters

There are many reasons for sending a thank-you letter. Only a small sample of letters can be included in this chapter, but there are some general guidelines that can be applied to almost any thank-you letter you might have to write:

- Do not forget to say thank you!

- Write promptly unless there are good reasons why you cannot do so, such as illness or bereavement. It is important to show that you are not taking a gift, help, good wishes, etc for granted.

- Informal thank-you letters, e.g. to friends and family, should whenever possible be handwritten, to give them a personal touch. On the other hand, if you are writing to thank someone on behalf of an organisation, your letter should be slightly more formal, in which case it would be better typed. Email may be convenient for an informal thank you when you want to deliver your thanks promptly or over a long distance and traditional 'snail' mail would take too long.

- Thank-you letters needn't be long. Be short and to the point. The relative formality or informality of the letter and your relationship to the recipient will dictate how much and what you say: you would naturally say more in a chatty letter to your aunt thanking her for a birthday present than you would in a letter to Lady Forbes-Smyth thanking her for opening the village fete.

- There is no right or wrong way to express thanks so long as you mean it. Be sincere in what you say (unless, of course, you are obliged to be insincerely grateful for the sake of politeness, in which case your aim is to make the other person believe you are sincere!).

- At the informal end of the spectrum of thank-you letters you can use notepaper, correspondence cards (see page 62), notelets or even postcards. More formal letters should not be written on notelets or postcards.

NOTE: Bear in mind the points discussed in Chapters 1 and 2. In the examples that follow, addresses and dates will be omitted for space reasons.

Presents

It is possible to buy pre-printed thank-you letters or cards, in which all you have to do is fill in the blanks with people's names and the details of the presents received. These are far too impersonal – and lazy – for proper thank-you letters; even for children, there are better alternatives (see page 77). If someone has made the effort to select, buy, wrap and send a present, the least you can do is write an individual personalised thank you.

When thanking someone for a present, mention the present by name (i.e. 'Thank you for the lovely socks', not just 'Thank you for your lovely present'). This sounds more appreciative, and shows that you actually care enough to remember what the present was. Here is one example of a thank-you letter to a close relative:

Dear Gran,

This is just a little note to thank you ever so much for the beautiful necklace you sent me as a graduation present. It's perfect. Really gorgeous. Did you realise the stones exactly matched the colour of my eyes? Yes, I expect you did. Knowing you, I bet you spent absolutely ages looking for just the right necklace with the colour of stones you wanted.

It's still hard to grasp that I've come to the end of my university years. It seems no time at all since I left school. I've had a great

*time at uni, and made some good friends, and I really did enjoy
my course, but now at last, no more exams, not ever again!
Whoopee!! I've had enough of the midnight slog.*

*I'm glad you're coming to stay with us next month. I was really
too busy swotting when you were here at New Year. This time, I'll
still be on holiday, as I don't start my new job till September, so we
can spend the whole two weeks together. Fabulous!*

Till then, take care.

*All my love,
  Julia*

Wedding or anniversary presents

Traditionally, wedding gifts were sent to the bride's home, and it was the
bride who replied on behalf of herself and her husband. Nowadays it is
quite normal for the couple to share the job of thanking friends and relatives for the gifts they have received. The same is also true for wedding
anniversary presents. Here is one example:

Dear Mr and Mrs Culpepper,

*Thank you very much for the beautiful set of wine glasses you
gave Ian and me as a wedding present. They were an excellent
choice, and I hope you won't get the wrong idea about Ian and me
and our future lifestyle if I say that we intend to make good use of
them!*

*It was so nice to meet you at our wedding. Ian had often spoken
about you, and I had been very much looking forward to making
your acquaintance. And weren't we lucky with the weather! With
such a wet summer, it was almost a miracle that we had such a
gorgeous sunny day.*

With thanks again for your lovely present, and your good wishes,

*Yours sincerely,
  Hazel*

Some useful phrases

- On behalf of . . . and myself, I am writing to thank you for . . .

- . . . joins with me in thanking you for the . . .

- . . . and I are writing to thank you for the . . . [In this case, both spouses sign the letter.]

- I know I have already said thank you for your beautiful wedding present, but I just wanted to write a brief note to you to say how much . . . and I appreciate the . . . you gave us.

- I look forward to meeting you on the . . .

- With thanks again, . . .

- With thanks again from . . . and myself for your delightful present, . . .

Leaving/retirement presents and parties

If you are writing to thank former colleagues for a leaving present and celebration, address the envelope to the most senior member of staff who was present (your head of department, line manager, director, etc). Address him or her by name (by first name or else by title and surname, whichever is appropriate) in the salutation, but include all your former colleagues in your thanks:

Dear Mr Carson,

   I am writing to thank you and all the staff at Bognor Brothers for the party you held in my honour last Friday, and also for the beautiful snooker cue you presented me with as a leaving gift.

   As I said in my speech on Friday, I've really enjoyed my twenty years at Bognor Brothers. It has been a very pleasant place to work, with staff and management always acting together as a team. While I must admit that I won't mind not having to come to work on a Monday morning, I will miss being part of that team.

I look forward to seeing you all again at the annual Christmas party, where for the first time I will be one of the 'former members of staff'. It will be a strange feeling.

My wife joins with me in thanking all of you at Bognor Brothers for a most enjoyable evening on Friday.

> *Yours sincerely,*
> *Charlie Dobson*

Weddings, parties and hospitality

The style of letter you write depends, of course, on your relationship with the person you are thanking. A letter to a friend's aunt and uncle whom you hardly know but who kindly put you up overnight for the friend's wedding would be a little more formal than a letter to your best friend and his partner who invited you round to a great dinner party.

Weddings

A letter of thanks written after attending a wedding reception should usually be sent to the hosts, but if you prefer it may be sent to the newly-weds themselves. It should be handwritten, on paper, a correspondence card, etc as appropriate (i.e. something that matches the wedding invitation in style and formality). Formal thanks can be expressed very briefly, but you can if you wish include some more conversational comment so that your letter is not too formal and impersonal:

> *Dear Mr and Mrs Harvey,*
> *William and I would like to thank you once again for your kind invitation to Kate and David's wedding and wedding reception.*
> *We had a most enjoyable day, and it was good to meet you and the other members of Kate and David's families. Even the rain*

did not spoil the occasion, and we found that sharing umbrellas
was a good way of getting to know the other guests!
William and I hope we will meet you again some day.

Yours sincerely,
Lauren Forbes

Dinner parties

If you have been at a party or dinner, it is good to make a point of mentioning some feature of the gathering that you especially enjoyed or
appreciated, such as the food, the atmosphere, the chance to meet the
other guests – anything that made the event particularly pleasant or
memorable:

My dear Maria,
Thank you so much for inviting Thomas and me to join you
and your family in celebrating your 75th birthday.
We had a lovely time with you yesterday. The meal was beautiful,
and it was wonderful to see you with your whole family gathered
round you. To think that Laura and Fred and the children came all
the way from New Zealand to be with you! (But then, how could they
not want to be with you on this special day? And the young folk are so
much more used to travelling than we were – I don't suppose it
seemed such a colossal journey to them as it does to me.)
It was such a good idea for you all to be spending this week all
together at the hotel. I hope the weather is as good with you as it
is here. You and the family will be up in the hills by now, I
imagine, just like you and the boys used to be most weekends. You
can probably still walk the younger ones off their feet!
Thomas and I will look forward to seeing all your photographs
when you get back.

With thanks again, and much love,
Catherine

Children's parties

You might want to write to thank someone on behalf of your child who has been to a party (but why not encourage the child to write something themselves – see below, page 77):

Dear Yvonne,

Thank you so much for inviting Jenny to Emma's party. It was her very first party, and she was so excited about going. And she clearly had a wonderful time – when she came back, she was just bursting to tell me all about it. The games, the cake, the clown, and of course the prize she won for pinning the tail on the donkey! She loved every minute of it, and she hasn't stopped talking about it since!

I think it's wonderful that there are still some parents who are prepared to organise traditional children's parties, and my husband says that when he picked Jenny up after the party it was obvious from the children's faces how much they had enjoyed Emma's.

I hope the party we'll be giving for Jenny next month will be as successful as Emma's. And we look forward to having Emma here with all Jenny's other friends.

With thanks again,
Rosemary

Hospitality

Dear Mr and Mrs Pagett,

Now that John and I are back home again, I wanted to write to you at once to say how much we appreciated your hospitality over the weekend. Although we had never met before, you really made us feel at home and part of the family. It was as if we had known each other for years.

I hope it wasn't too much inconvenience for you to have two more people in the house when there was so much to do before the wedding. And we really didn't expect you to cook a beautiful meal for us on Friday night. It was very kind of you.

Please do come and stay with us any time you're in this part of England. Now, I really mean that, I am not just saying it to be polite. John and I look on you as friends now, and friends are always welcome here.

With thanks again, and best wishes from both of us,
Jane

Other events

Dear Miss Osborne,

I would like to thank you and the other members of the Gala committee once again for inviting me to judge this year's flower show. I felt very honoured to have been asked to do so.

It was an absolute delight for me to judge the displays, and I was very impressed by the standard of the flowers on show, particularly in view of the appalling weather we have had this summer.

Thank you also for the beautiful vase I was presented with. I shall treasure it as a memento of a most enjoyable day.

Yours sincerely,
Janet Hudson

Thanks for assistance

If you get assistance or advice from someone, don't just say thank you for it: tell them in your letter what they helped to achieve.

The first letter is an official thank you, and it is therefore appropriate to type it, though a handwritten letter would be just as acceptable:

Dear Mrs Hudson,

On behalf of the gala committee, I would like to thank you for judging the flower show at this year's gala.

The gala was a great success, and we were lucky that the weather was kind to us. Considering the wet summer we have had, the quality of the flowers on show was quite amazing. I really don't know how you could make a decision between so many wonderful displays. I don't think I could have!

As you know, the profits from this year's gala are going to the local hospice, and although we have not finalised the accounts, it seems that we will be able to give them a cheque for something in the region of £3000. A very satisfactory result, and we would like to thank you again for your part in the success of the event.

Yours sincerely,
Tessa Osborne

The next letter is more informal than the previous one, and therefore would be better handwritten, Again, it is important not just to say thank you, but to go a bit beyond that to make the letter more personal:

Dear Mrs Cornwell,

I know we have spoken on the phone several times since Dad had his fall, but I do want to write to you to thank you once again for all you have done for him in the past couple of weeks. It has made the situation so much easier for my sister and myself, living far away from Dad as we both do, to know that he had a neighbour keeping an eye on him while he recovered. And doing his shopping! And feeding him! (He loves your chicken, tomato and tarragon soup, and raves about your apple and pear pie. I must get the recipes from you one day.)

Dad has mentioned that you are a keen gardener, so Janice and I would like to give you this garden token to show our appreciation for all you have been doing for Dad. I hope you will

*find something that will give you a lot of pleasure in your garden
in the years to come.*

With best wishes and once again our thanks,

Yours,
Moira Smart

Some useful phrases

- I am writing to thank you for . . .
- . . . send you our heartfelt thanks for . . .
- . . . extend our sincere/heartfelt thanks to . . .
- . . . express to you our thanks . . .
- Please accept our sincere thanks for . . .
- Please thank . . . for me.
- Please convey to . . . my sincere thanks for . . .
- . . . wish to express my appreciation for . . .
- . . . was greatly appreciated.
- I very much appreciated . . .
- . . . wish to express to you my gratitude for . . .
- . . . can hardly find the words to express our gratitude . . .

Children's thank-you letters

While it is perhaps going beyond the remit of this book to say that, in
this time of declining standards in courtesy, parents should encourage

children to write thank-you letters, we can at least suggest some ways in which children might do this.

One possibility is to use pre-printed thank-you letters or cards, in which all the child has to do is fill in the blanks with names and the details of the present. These are perhaps acceptable for children who are able to write but too young to write much, but older children should certainly be encouraged to write proper (even if short) letters instead.

However, there is a lot of scope for creativity, allowing even preschool children to express their thanks for presents received or parties attended. The key point is not that someone should receive a well-written, perfectly grammatical and accurately spelt letter, but that they receive *something* that shows the child's appreciation.

If a child is too young to write a thank you, they could draw a picture instead. For example, if a young child has been at a friend's birthday party, an adult could write or print a simple little letter saying:

> *Dear Lisa,*
> *Thank you for inviting me to your party. I really enjoyed it. I liked the bouncy castle the best.*
>
> *Love,*
> *Ellie*

while Ellie could add a few scratchy kisses after her name and draw a picture of herself on the bouncy castle below the letter. Not a lot of effort for the parent, but enough effort by the child to show her appreciation (and to teach her to show appreciation). Similarly, if a little girl gets a dress for her birthday from her aunt and uncle, she could draw a picture of herself wearing it as her thank you. If a child is sent money as a present, they could draw a picture of what they bought with it (and if that might not be clear enough to the sender of the money, you could take a photograph of the child playing with the new toy and send that as well – photography is a useful adjunct to children's thank-you letters). Even a child's simple drawing of a happy smiling face could be enough for a thank you, with an adult 'topping and tailing' the letter with 'Dear . . .', 'Thank you' and 'Love, . . .'.

Another way of helping a pre-school child write a thank you is for an adult to write a short note by outlining the letter shapes in dots, which the child can then draw over in a 'join-the-dots' fashion. In this case, a little more time and effort is involved on the part of the adult, but it can make young children feel very grown up to be really writing their own thank-you letters.

8 Congratulations

An engagement, a new baby, an exam success or driving test passed, a new job or promotion, perhaps a public honour for a lifetime's work: there are many reasons to offer someone your congratulations. And a well-written letter will make your congratulations a little more special.

Letters of congratulations may be informal or formal, depending on who you are writing to. You can write a short and fairly conversational note to a friend or relative, but a more formal letter is required if you are writing to someone more eminent or with whom you are less well acquainted. It may be that, as the chairperson or secretary of a club or association, you are called on to offer someone congratulations on behalf of the whole membership; this would almost certainly require a formal letter, though the level of formality would depend on the recipient: a letter to a member of the group might be rather less formal than a letter to someone who did not belong to the group.

NOTE: Congratulatory letters should have the general format of formal or informal letters (see Chapters 1 and 2). In the examples that follow, addresses and dates will be omitted to save space on the page.

A letter of congratulations need not be long. If it is too long, it may sound forced and insincere. Keep the following points in mind:

- Write promptly, as soon as you are aware of the person's success.

- Even if you have seen the person and congratulated them face to face, a further letter or note is not inappropriate. They will appreciate the extra effort you have made.

- Express your pleasure at the person's success, but never in terms that might suggest surprise (you don't want to give the impression that you didn't think they were capable of achieving their success or don't think they deserve it).

- Do not mention anything negative. Focus only on the positive. For example, if a student gets an Upper Second degree, you congratulate them on that; you do not say it's a pity they didn't get a First.

- Avoid excessive flattery. You will probably want to say that the success was deserved, but don't make a meal of it. That sounds insincere.

- Avoid expressing any hint of envy or jealousy (even facetiously) at the other person's success. This letter is about them, not about you.

- Should the person you are congratulating have reached a position of some seniority or authority or have been appointed to a public office, do not (again, not even facetiously) suggest that they are now in a position to help you in some way.

- Similarly, in a business context, while a well-worded and timely letter of congratulations to a business associate may make them more favourable to future business dealings with you, you must not write anything to suggest you are expecting this. This is not the time to talk business.

- If the person you are writing to has been appointed to a new position, you may, on the other hand, offer your help and support to them in their new role.

- You may wish the other person success in their new role or position, but do not wish them 'good luck', which might give the impression either that you are questioning their competence or ability or that you think they have been handed a poisoned chalice and will need all the luck they can get.

- Lastly, be careful about sending congratulations in situations where the recipient might not want to be congratulated. For example, a person who has recently reached retirement age and been obliged to leave a job that has given them satisfaction and a clear role in life may be feeling anxious and uncertain rather than positive about the future. Congratulations may not be in order. Some acknowledgement of their changed role and status may be appropriate, but give careful thought to what you want to say and how you want to say it.

Nowadays, there are of course cards available in shops for almost every congratulatory situation: new baby, new house, new job, engagement, retirement, etc. These are, however, only suitable as replacements for informal letters. More formal situations require letters. And even if you send a card, you might want to add a brief note expressing your congratulations in your own words:

Dear Mary,

I was very pleased to hear from your mother that you have got your place at Oxford. Well done! A fitting reward for all the hard work I know you have put in over the past two years at 6th form college.

I'm sure you will enjoy your time at Magdalen – I know I did, so many years ago – and I know you will do as well at university as you have done at school. I look forward to hearing how you get on.

Uncle Bill and Ian send their congratulations too.

Love,
Auntie Fran

The following two letters are more formal, even though in the second case the two people clearly know each other:

Dear Mr West,

I have just read in this morning's Times that you have been awarded an OBE for services to education in the New Year Honours list, and I would like to offer you my congratulations and say that in my opinion the recognition you have now received is very well deserved and long overdue.

It is some years now since my two sons, James and Mark

Goodall, attended Barton Grange College, at a time when it was
going through a somewhat troubled and uncertain period in its
development. During those difficult years, my wife and I, along with
many other parents of Barton Grange students, were grateful for the
wisdom, leadership, vision and courage you showed as you steered
the college forward to become the educational success that we knew
it could, and should, be. It is without a doubt thanks to you that the
college has the high standing that it enjoys today, and for that students and parents in the area owe you a huge debt of gratitude. It is
good to see that the country has now acknowledged this debt.

Yours sincerely,

[signature here]

Robert Goodall

Dear Philip,
On behalf of the office-bearers and members of the North
Landerton Liberal Democrats, I am writing to offer you our
congratulations on your election as Convenor of Landerton
District Council.
You have put in many years of hard work in the service of the
people of Landerton, and we are glad to see that this has been
recognised and duly rewarded by your fellow-councillors.
You can, of course, be sure of our support in all that you
undertake in your new capacity.
With best wishes,

Yours sincerely,

[signature here]

Kenneth Quigley
Chairperson, North Wessex Liberal Democrats

Some useful phrases

- Many congratulations on . . .

- I am writing to send/offer you our congratulations . . .

- . . . would like to add my congratulations . . .

- . . . send you heartiest congratulations . . .

- Please accept our congratulations . . .

- Allow me to offer you my congratulations . . .

- . . . extend our warmest congratulations . . .

- . . . my most sincere congratulations . . .

- . . . would like to congratulate you on . . .

- . . . would like to say well done on . . .

- . . . would like to say how pleased/delighted I was to hear of . . .

9 Bad news, sympathy and condolences

In letters conveying bad news, sympathy or condolences, there is particular need for tact and sensitivity, for care over both *what* is said and *how* it is said. You do not want to write anything that will cause the recipient distress or add to the distress they are already feeling. And that makes these letters probably the most difficult letters anyone ever has to write.

Letters conveying bad news, sympathy or condolences may vary from the fairly informal to the quite formal, depending on the circumstances and on your relationship with the person or people involved. However, even at the more formal end of the spectrum, for example if you were sending your condolences to someone such as a business acquaintance whom you do not know well or intimately, you should nevertheless try to give your letter a personal touch.

And since such letters, even to people you hardly know, are personal letters, they should be handwritten.

Be realistic

One reason that many people find it difficult to write letters breaking bad news or offering condolences is that they set themselves unrealistic goals. Of course you don't want to cause unnecessary distress, but you may not be able to avoid causing *some* distress: a letter that brings seriously bad news may well upset the person who reads it, and there is nothing you can do about that; a letter to someone who has recently been bereaved may contain words of comfort and support, but they may still become upset when reading it. The upset itself is part of the healing process.

Some letters of sympathy are of course easier to write than others, depending on the situation: a broken leg, for example, is hardly as serious as a terminal illness. In some cases, therefore, your letter could be light-hearted and even humorous in a way that would obviously be totally inappropriate in other situations.

But the worst thing you could do is not write at all.

Tactics

Since letters like these are not easy to write, it is all too easy to put off writing them. But these are letters that really must be written promptly.

The more difficult the letter, the less you should worry in the first instance about what to say: just get something down on paper. Brainstorm – words, notes, feelings, memories, any ideas at all. Once you have made a start, you can alter and improve what you have written; until you make a start, all you have is a blank sheet of paper. Don't wait for inspiration: as most writers know, the words you need generally come while you are writing, not before.

Breaking bad news

Bad news comes in many forms, and we cannot deal with them all in this book. Perhaps the worst kind of bad news is that of someone's death, and we will take that as our main theme in this section.

With so many arrangements to be made after a death and so many people to contact, no one will expect a long letter from you. The exact content of the letter will of course depend on the circumstances: was the death expected or sudden, and if expected, how much was the person you are writing to already aware of the situation?

In announcing deaths, letters come somewhere between public notices in newspapers and personal telephone calls. On the one hand, many people would not expect any direct notification from you, and for them a letter is unnecessary (newspaper announcements and word of mouth are enough); on the other hand, close friends and relatives might expect to hear the news from you personally (i.e. by phone), and for them a letter might not be appropriate. It is quite possible that there is no one to whom you would write an informal letter, while letters to the deceased person's lawyer, insurance companies, and so on would be short, formal and businesslike. For the purposes of this chapter, however, let us assume that there are some relatives or acquaintances that you want to write to, in a fairly informal style:

> *Dear Harriet,*
>
> *I'm afraid I am writing to you with some very sad news.*
>
> *You know from my letter last Christmas that Dad had a stroke at the end of last year. He seemed to recover from it, and the doctors were very pleased with his progress, although he was never quite his old self again. Sadly, he had another stroke last Tuesday, and I am sorry to say that he passed away, peacefully, in hospital yesterday morning.*
>
> *The funeral arrangements haven't been fixed yet, but I expect the funeral will take place sometime early next week at the local Methodist church (where Dad was, of course, a lifelong member). I will be in touch again to confirm the details as soon as possible. There will be a reception somewhere nearby after the funeral.*
>
> *If you are coming to the funeral, please do come and stay with me. You mustn't think of going to a hotel. It would be lovely to see you again after so long, even in these sad circumstances.*
>
> *With much love,*
> *Betty*

Details that may need to be included in your letter, or in a follow-up letter once the arrangements have been made, are:

- where and when the funeral will take place;

- whether there are to be flowers, and if so whether only from close family;

- whether donations are to be made, perhaps in lieu of flowers, to a charity, hospital, hospice, etc;

- whether there will be a reception after the funeral, and if so where.

It will make the letter more personal if you are able to refer to something in the past that relates the person to whom you are writing to the person whose death you are writing about. For example: 'I know you were one of Dad's closest friends . . .', 'My father often talked about the time you and he spent together in the army . . .', etc. The same applies if you are having to break bad news of a serious or terminal illness.

NOTE: In the previous example and those that follow, the writer's address and the dates are omitted only for space reasons. Letters should have the structure and layout outlined in Chapter 1.

A letter to the deceased person's lawyer can be much briefer. As a business letter, it need not be handwritten, and it should have the full style appropriate to a business letter (see page 107). The key points for the letter are that you clearly identify the person who has died and your relationship to them, and state the place and date of their death. Other matters such as death certificates and wills, though necessary, can be dealt with at a later time:

Mr I Sanderson
Murphy, Sanderson & Partners
23 Hill Place
Ashford
GE19 5JU

Dear Mr Sanderson,

<u>*Death of Mr John Simmons, 14 Harrow Court, Ashford*</u>

I am writing to inform you of the death of my father, John Simmons, last Wednesday, 4th August 2010, at St Margaret's Hospital, Ashford.

I will telephone you in the next few days to arrange a suitable time for me to come to your office to deal with the necessary formalities.

Yours sincerely,

[**signature here**]

Elizabeth Coombs (Mrs)

A letter to an organisation the deceased person belonged to should be similarly brief:

The Oak Woods Protection Society,
34 Potters Road,
Norton,
NR17 8TR

Dear Sirs,

<u>*Death of Mr John Simmons, 14 Harrow Court, Ashford*</u>
<u>*Membership No.: 740165JS*</u>

I am writing to inform you of the recent death of my father, John Simmons, who was a member of your Society.

I would be grateful if you would remove his name from your membership and mailing lists.

Thank you for your assistance.

Yours faithfully,

[**signature here**]

Elizabeth Coombs (Mrs)

Other bad news

To complete this section, here are a couple of letters breaking other bad news:

> *Dear Miriam,*
>
> *I'm sorry to have to write to you with some bad news.*
>
> *I can't think of any easy way to say this, so I will simply let you know the situation we are in. John was knocked down by a hit-and-run driver yesterday afternoon as he was coming back from the bowling green. He is in hospital in a coma, and I'm afraid the doctors are not hopeful about his recovery. He has some brain damage and damage to other organs, as well as a few broken bones. At any age, this would be very serious; at John's age, the doctors are warning me that it may prove fatal.*
>
> *I am writing this at the hospital, because I may not have a chance to phone over the next few days. Actually, I'm not sure I could cope with phoning round everyone to pass on the news, and in any case writing letters keeps my mind occupied while I am here. I'd like to have waited until the doctors were more certain about how things will go, but I thought I ought to let you know straight away what has happened, and how John is. I'll keep you posted.*
>
> *With much love,*
> *Ann*

> *Dear Mum and Dad,*
>
> *You'll be surprised to be getting a letter from me, but I just can't face phoning you right now with the news I have to tell you. I think it would be better if you had time to take it in before we speak.*
>
> *You must have realised that things have not been right between Richard and me recently. It's not something we have*

been able to hide very well. Well, we finally sat down and talked it over last night, and I'm afraid we've decided to split up. Neither of us can see any future for our marriage, and we both feel it's time to admit, to ourselves and to everyone else, that it just isn't working and that we would both be happier if we separated. And it's not a trial separation, our marriage is definitely over.

I know how much this news will upset you. I know how very fond of Richard you are. So am I still in a way, but not in a way that can make our marriage work, and he feels the same about me. We would rather part as friends now than drag this on any longer till perhaps we can't stand the sight of each other.

Anyhow, that's the sad news. Please don't phone me when you read this letter. I'll be in touch in a couple of days.

Richard and I are so sorry this has happened, but really it is for the best.

Love,
Dee

Sympathy and condolences

Letters of sympathy or condolence are better kept short, as those reading them may not be in a fit mental state to wade through long letters. People who find themselves or a loved one seriously ill or who are recently bereaved may be in a state of shock. What they need is a brief letter offering sympathy, comfort and support.

If the illness or disability is not severe, and the person is likely to recover, your letter can be upbeat and even humorous. Letters like this cause no problems. The difficult letters are those you have to write to someone who is severely (and possibly terminally) ill or permanently disabled, or to someone who is facing up to such a condition in a close and much-loved relative or partner, or to someone who has been recently bereaved. There are some useful guidelines to keep in mind:

- Even though these letters are hard to write, it is important that you do write, and promptly. The bereaved and seriously ill can feel very isolated and your failure to write because you 'don't know what to say' or it 'might make them feel worse' could make them feel even more alone.

- Do not shy away from the bad news. Acknowledge it openly and then move on to something more positive.

- Do not try to say too much and get lost in words. Keep it short and simple.

- Be yourself, be natural. Use normal, everyday language. Do not adopt a falsely solemn or pious tone. The person you are writing to wants to hear from you as they know you.

- Do not talk about the meaning or unfairness of life. They can probably do without philosophy at this point.

- You do not have to offer advice, and probably you shouldn't; certainly do not tell people to 'keep their chin up' or use other similar pointless recommendations.

- Watch out for clichés, platitudes and flat, hackneyed phrases. They bring no comfort to anyone.

- Do if possible offer practical help and support. Put yourself in the other person's situation and think of their needs. Remember that people may not just need help now but three or six months on as well. It can be reassuring to be told that an offer of help is not just for the next couple of weeks.

Experts in counselling often stress two things you should *not* do in these circumstances:

- Do not say you know how the other person feels. You don't.

- Do not talk about someone else you know who was in the same circumstances; the focus must be on the person you are writing to.

Expressing sympathy when the details are unknown

If you have been told that someone is ill, but not how ill, be careful what you say. Obviously you should express hopes for recovery, but it is wise not to be too cheerful and humorous about the situation in case they are more seriously ill than you are aware. Keep it short, keep it general:

> *Dear John,*
> *We have just heard at this evening's practice that you are not very well at the moment, and the choir have asked me to send you our very best wishes and hopes for a speedy recovery. The tenors need you back!*
>
> *Best wishes,*
> *Simon*

Expressing sympathy for a serious or terminal condition

You have learned that an acquaintance, a friend or a relative, or someone close to them, has either a long-term seriously debilitating illness or a terminal condition. They are facing the end of a life they have known, perhaps the end of life itself. How do you respond? What can you say?

To some extent it depends on what the person has said to you, and how they are coping with their changed situation. If you are responding to bad news, be sensitive to how it has been conveyed to you. But there are some general points to keep in mind:

- Your purpose in writing is to show that you care, and that you are there for the other person, and those around them, if they need your support.

- Say you are sorry or sad to hear the news. Some people feel that 'I was sorry to hear . . .' is a trite cliché to be avoided, but it isn't. No doubt you are sorry or sad, and you can say so. But avoid saying how upset you were – you don't want to make the other person feel down because you feel down. Be positive, avoid anything negative.

- There is always hope, but pretending the prognosis is better than it is helps nobody. Accept and acknowledge the situation openly and honestly. But don't dwell on it either: that would not be very uplifting.

- If you like, admit that it is difficult to know what to say.

- Do not talk about the person's life as if it was already over and in the past. Whether suffering from a long-term disability or a life-threatening illness, they still have more life to live. Be positive and upbeat.

- Similarly, someone in this situation may need reassurance that they are still valued, that as far as possible in the circumstances their lives will continue as before, and that they will still be welcome in activities, societies and groups they have taken part in before.

Here is one example of a suitable letter acknowledging bad news and offering support:

Dear John,

I was very sorry to hear from Marjory this morning that you are back in hospital again and that you have received some very bad news.

I admit I cannot easily find words to express my feelings at the moment. We know each other too well for me to sit here and write a string of platitudes, but you will know that I am thinking of you and that you and Marjory will be in my prayers today and in the days ahead.

Now, I know that Marjory doesn't drive and that visiting the hospital must therefore be difficult for her. I have spoken to the other members of the choir this evening and we are drawing up a rota of cars and drivers so that she will at least be spared all those awful bus journeys. I will be bringing her on Wednesday afternoon, and of course I will look in on you then. We'll also make sure that Marjory can get to the shops when she needs to. If there is anything else we can do to help, you know you and she only have to ask.

The choir all send you their best regards. We hope you'll be out of hospital soon, and that you'll be back with us again as soon as you feel able to. The tenors need you!

With best wishes,
Simon

Condolences

When it is a matter of someone's death, you may be an acquaintance or friend of both the deceased person and of the person you are writing to, or of only one of them; you may be close to them or not close to them, know them well or not well at all. You may have some idea what might comfort the bereaved person, or absolutely no idea. All this will affect what and how you write:

- Perhaps nothing you can say will help the bereaved person grieve less; you must obviously try to say nothing that will make them grieve more. But it is quite appropriate to express your own feelings of grief as well as acknowledging theirs.

- Obviously you will refer to the death – why else would you be writing? – but do not dwell on it. Avoid clichéd sentiments such as the death being 'a blessed release' or 'a sad end', or the person who has died having had 'a good innings'.

- Be supportive. You may want to say something that will reassure them of the positive role they have played in the deceased person's life and illness.

- If you knew the deceased, say what they meant to you. Write about some aspect of their character or achievements for which you liked and admired them and/or some shared occasion or experience you particularly remember. There is no need to avoid humour; one can grieve and laugh at the same time. In general, avoid negative thoughts and comments (though something mild along the lines of

'We didn't always agree but I always admired him' is all right), and never write anything you might later regret.

- Be careful if mentioning God, life after death, etc, unless you are sure of the bereaved person's beliefs or how they will feel if you refer to yours. Avoid bland platitudes ('gone to a better place') if they reflect neither your nor their beliefs.

Here is a sample letter of condolence:

Dear Virginia,

Sheila and I were very saddened when we read your letter this morning. Your father's death comes as a great shock to us both, and it is difficult to put into words what we are feeling right now. Even at this distance, his passing will leave a huge empty space in our lives, as it must also do in yours, and we will miss him terribly.

Strangely, my wife and I were talking about your father only yesterday. We saw a flock of waxwings in the garden, pecking at the berries (a sure sign that winter is here!), and we were remembering how pleased Leonard was when we saw some in the garden the last time he and your mother were here. He was always such a keen birdwatcher, and I have some wonderful memories, and photographs, of the birdwatching trips we had together, here and in Canada. I'll miss his knowledge, I'll miss his enthusiasm, and I'll even miss his terrible jokes!

As you rightly suspected, Sheila and I would not have managed to join you for Leonard's funeral. I'm afraid that crossing the Atlantic and most of Canada would have been just too much of a journey for us to contemplate these days. But today being the day of the funeral, our thoughts will be with you and Bob and Jim and your families as you say goodbye to Leonard and begin to come to terms with your sad loss.

With much love from Sheila and myself,
Tom Sanders

A letter of condolence to a business acquaintance is not strictly a business letter but a personal letter. It is best laid out in the style of a more informal letter (see page 3), but it may nonetheless have the name and business address of the person you are writing to above the salutation. The style and wording will depend on your relationship with the person you are writing to, and whether you are writing in a personal capacity or on behalf of your company or organisation. The letter can in either case be brief, but not so brief as to be cold and impersonal. If you are writing on behalf of an organisation, your letter will usually be typed:

Mr Charles Caldwell
Caldwell & Clarke plc
16 High Street
Boothborough
WQ21 7YT

Dear Mr Caldwell,

It was with great sadness that we at Bognor Brothers learned today of the sudden death of your partner, Thomas Clarke.

He was well respected by all of us in the paint-manufacturing industry as a man of both great knowledge and great integrity. Many of us were also fortunate to know him as a friend.

The directors and staff of Bognor Brothers join with me in sending you and your colleagues our sincere condolences.

Yours sincerely,

[signature here]

William Carson
CEO, Bognor Brothers plc

or less formally, a handwritten letter may be best:

> *Mr Charles Caldwell*
> *Caldwell & Clarke plc,*
> *16 High Street,*
> *Boothborough*
> *WQ21 7YT*
>
> *Dear Charles,*
>
> *I was very sorry to hear of Thomas's death this morning.*
>
> *As I am sure you are well aware, all of us in the paint-manufacturing industry held him in very high regard as a man of great knowledge and great integrity. He'll be sadly missed by all those who knew him as a colleague and as a good friend. Conferences just won't be the same without him – and his appalling puns!*
>
> *All of us at Bognor Brothers send you and your colleagues our sincere condolences.*
>
> *Yours sincerely,*
> *Bill*

Alternatives to letters

If you cannot find the right words for a letter, you might choose an appropriate card from the many available in shops. Then you can simply add a short personal message. Do try to write something in your own words – a card alone, while kind, is rather too impersonal.

If you really cannot think of anything to say, send a notelet or card with a short message. Even

> *Thinking of you at this sad time.*
>
> *With love,*
> *Emily Harper*

while perhaps unimaginative, is better than nothing at all and will let the recipient know of your feelings.

Some useful phrases

- We were very sad to hear . . .

- We were so sorry to hear . . .

- It was with deep/great sadness that we heard/read that . . . had passed away.

- We were deeply/greatly saddened to learn of the death of . . .

- I wish to extend/offer our deep/deepest/sincere sympathy on your sad loss.

- We send/extend/offer our deepest condolences . . .

- Please accept our sincere condolences on . . .

- Please accept my sympathy on . . .

- This comes with our warmest love and deepest sympathy.

- With love and sympathy, . . .

Replying to letters of sympathy and condolence

When and how you reply to a letter of sympathy or condolence depends very much on circumstances. If you have been bereaved, you may receive many cards and letters of condolence. You may need some time to get over your loss before you can face writing about it or acknowledging these expressions of sympathy. This is one occasion when it is quite acceptable for thank-you letters not to be written immediately.

Your letter can be brief or not, as you choose. If the person you are replying to has shared memories of the deceased person in their letter, you may want to refer to them and perhaps add memories of your own. This is a good time to remember the good times. But if you want something shorter, here is a specimen to base your reply on:

Dear Muriel,

Thank you for your kind and thoughtful letter. I so much appreciated you writing to give me your sympathy and support. It brings me great comfort to know that you are thinking of me at this sad time. I'll phone you soon.

> *Love,*
> *Mary*

10 Love letters

Since the title of this book is *Perfect Letters and Emails for _All_ Occasions*, perhaps something needs to be said about love letters. Even if you are not normally a letter-writer, even if you see the love of your life every day, you must surely at some point put pen to paper and tell him or her how you feel. But really – do you need *our* help to do this? Well, if you're looking at this chapter, perhaps you do (or think you do).

Love letters are the most personal of personal letters, so they should in general be handwritten. Typing is too impersonal for letters of this sort. Of course there are exceptions to this rule: if you are far apart and you want to keep up regular and quick written communication with each other, email has its uses (as well as the benefit of being much cheaper than long passionate phone calls!).

Email animations and backgrounds

It must also be admitted that in terms of presentation the internet does have a lot to offer. If you go online, you will find various sites that can provide you with amusing animations, clip-art and interesting backgrounds that you can add to emails, and if you think these will enhance your message, then use them. But the illustrations and fancy backgrounds aren't a substitute for your message, they are only embellishments.

And there is still a need for a good love *letter* as well – even if you email regularly, you should express your feelings in a letter sometime.

What to say?

You may be writing to the love of your life, or to someone you hope will be one day. You will probably be writing to someone you know quite well; however, it may be that you do not know them well at all (but hope to). More than with any other type of letter, with love letters there is only a little help that can be given in any book, because these letters are so personal and the circumstances so varied. This chapter can only touch on the main broad principles.

How should you begin your letter? 'Dear Ruth' is safe, if a bit tame; 'My dearest darling wonderful Ruth' would get a bit closer to making Ruth feel special, but perhaps it's not entirely right when writing to someone you hardly yet know. 'Dear Flopsy Bunny' is fine if you know Ruth likes being called 'Flopsy Bunny' but a no-no if you are not sure. Only you can decide what is appropriate.

Next you have to decide what you are going to say. Well, what do you want to say? What is the point of your letter? A night of passion or a lifetime of love (or both)? Are you asking someone to love you, or thanking them because they do? You should obviously express your feelings for the person you are writing to. Say what it is that makes you love them. Describe how you feel when you are with them, and how you feel when you are apart. You might describe where you are, and imagine where they are and what they will be doing at that moment. Perhaps say how you felt when you first saw or met them, and how they have changed your life. Tell them how often you think of them, and what it is you think about. Say what you remember about times you have spent together, and what you are looking forward to in the days, weeks, months, years ahead. Commitment and reassurance are important – tell them that they are loved and wanted and always will be. Thank them for loving you (if they do). Tell them how you would feel if you ever split up. In short, say all that is in your mind and in your heart. Make them laugh, make them cry, but let them know you are thinking of them, and make them think of you. Be honest, be open – and be natural, just be yourself.

If you really can't think what to say, you could use quotations, song lyrics, poetry, and so on (but don't overdo it – what you write should be, for the most part, *your* words, not a string of quotations from someone else). You could quote words from a favourite song or a favourite poem: for example, you could say 'Just as our song says, "I feel like I'm on a dark island when I'm not with you".' You could also try writing poetry yourself – it might not win prizes, but it might win hearts!

If you are still stuck for ideas, then go online. There are many useful sites to help you: just google 'love letters' or something similar. You will find websites with hundreds of ideas for what to say, how to say it, and how to make it special. Take these and develop them into something unique.

Examples from the experts

Many books of love letters have been published, setting out for all to read the heartfelt longings, intimate passions, cautious hopes and secret confidences written by the rich and famous (and sometimes the not-so-rich or not-so-famous) to husbands, wives, partners and lovers. Many of these letters are a joy to read, and the following is a beautiful example of a love letter, one of many sent by Napoleon Bonaparte to his future wife Josephine.

Paris, December 1795

I wake filled with thoughts of you. Your portrait and the intoxicating evening which we spent yesterday have left my senses in turmoil. Sweet, incomparable Josephine, what a strange effect you have on my heart! Are you angry? Do I see you looking sad? Are you worried? . . . My soul aches with sorrow, and there can be no rest for your lover; but is there still more in store for me when, yielding to the profound feelings which overwhelm me, I draw from your lips, from your heart a love which consumes me with fire? Ah! it was last night that I fully realised how false an image of you your portrait gives!

You are leaving at noon; I shall see you in three hours.

*Until then, mio dolce amor, a thousand kisses; but give me none
in return, for they set my blood on fire.*

And this letter is from the 19th-century French actress Juliette Drouet to
the author and dramatist Victor Hugo:

*If only I were a clever woman, I could describe to you, my
gorgeous bird, how you unite in yourself the beauties of form,
plumage and song!*

*I would tell you that you are the greatest marvel of all ages, and I
should only be speaking the simple truth. But to put all this into
suitable words, my superb one, I should require a voice far more
harmonious than that which is bestowed upon my species – for I
am the humble owl that you mocked at only lately; therefore, it
cannot be.*

*I will not tell you to what degree you are dazzling and
resplendent; I leave that to the birds of sweet song who, as you
know, are none the less beautiful and appreciative.*

*I am content to delegate to them the duty of watching, listening
and admiring, while to myself I reserve the right of loving; this
may be less attractive to the ear, but it is sweeter far to the heart.*

*I love you, I love you, my Victor; I can not reiterate it too often;
I can never express it as much as I feel it.*

*I recognise you in all the beauty that surrounds me – in form, in
colour, in perfume, in harmonious sound: all of these mean you
to me. You are superior to them all.*

*You are not only the solar spectrum with the seven luminous
colours, but the sun himself, that illumines, warms, and*

revivifies! This is what you are, and I am the lowly woman that
adores you.

Juliette

Finally, there's this simple note from Samuel Langhorne Clemens
(better known by his pen-name Mark Twain) to his future wife Olivia
Langdon:

Out of the depths of my happy heart wells a great tide of love and
prayer for this priceless treasure that is confided to my life-long
keeping.

You cannot see its intangible waves as they flow towards you,
darling, but in these lines you will hear, as it were, the distant
beating of the surf.

Be creative – think outside the box

Of course, in the field of love letters, you need not limit yourself to a
letter alone. In fact, you needn't write a conventional letter at all. Be cre-
ative. What would be *really* special? Obviously having your letter delivered with a bunch of her favourite flowers or a six-pack of his favourite
beer is good, but could you think up something more out of the ordin-
ary? Creativity lets you say less and convey more. Here are a few ideas:

• Once you have written your letter, tear it up and hide small parts in
  different places around the house/flat for your loved one to find. Or
  open up a box of chocolates and hide your message in small pieces
  under each of the chocolates.

• Instead of a letter, you could write down all the things you love about
  your partner on slips of perfumed paper, maybe cut into heart
  shapes, put these messages in a pretty box and give them that.

- Find eight different bottles of wine or beer, eight different bottles of perfume, eight different brands of chocolate or cake, or eight of anything else appropriate, with initial letters that spell out 'I love you'. Or choose any other appropriate message and a corresponding number of objects to spell it out.

- Make up a list of things you love about them based on the letters of their name or both your names.

- You could send your love message in a bottle with a ribbon round it or with a red rose attached. Even better, if you know you are going for a walk on a beach, hide the bottle and 'find' it again during the walk.

- Open up a tub of ice-cream and write your message on the ice-cream in melted chocolate or strawberry sauce. Put the lid back on again, and bring out the tub at a suitable moment.

- You could go to a studio and record a song that expresses your feelings.

- If you are artistic, or even if you are not, how about expressing your feelings in a picture?

Go for it!

Whatever you decide to do, make sure that you're honest and you speak from the heart. And – remember to send it! Lurking at the back of drawers all over the country are half-finished letters or notes that were never posted. It's true that you can't tell how your letter will be received, and it's equally true that there are sometimes very good reasons not to send a message. But if you really feel that you want to express yourself, then our advice would be to go for it.

11 Business letters, faxes and memos

Business letters

Business letters are one type of formal letter, more standardised in structure than other formal letters and with their own specific conventions:

- If possible, business letters should be typed rather than handwritten.

- You would normally use the blocked layout (see page 11) for business letters, especially if they are typed.

- The name and address of the recipient are always included (as in the letter on page 10).

- The date should be written out as on any other letter. Do not write 'Date as postmark'. (Postmarks are not always clear; and anyway, who keeps envelopes?)

- A business letter should have a heading that allows the recipient to see at once what the letter is about (see the example on page 11).

- A business letter may include reference codes that the sender and the recipient use to file and keep track of their correspondence (see the letter from Anis Printer Supplies on page 15). Reference codes are not obligatory in business correspondence: if you are an individual rather than a company, you do not have to create a reference code for your letter; but if you receive a letter from a company with a reference code on it, you should always include that code in any further correspondence.

For the attention of . . .

If you want your letter to be read and dealt with by a particular person in a company or organisation, you should name that person in a line below the name and address of the company or organisation:

Bognor Brothers plc
23 March Road
Boothton
WQ21 3XH

For the attention of Arthur Brown

Dear Sirs,
. . . . . .

'For the attention of' may be shortened to 'Attention:' or 'FAO:'.

When a letter is sent 'For the attention of' a particular person, it is considered correct to address the salutation either to the company (i.e. 'Dear Sirs') or to the person named (e.g. 'Dear Mr Brown').

Signing a letter 'pp'

A business letter may be signed on behalf of the sender by someone else, such as a secretary or personal assistant. In this case, the person signing the letter uses their own name, but adds the abbreviation 'pp' before the name of the person on whose behalf they are writing:

. . . . . .
Yours sincerely,

[signature here]
pp Trevor Jones

Marketing Director

There are two opinions on the correct use of 'pp':

* If 'pp' is taken to stand for the Latin phrase *per procurationem* ('through the agency of'), then it should precede the signature:

  . . . . . .

  Yours sincerely,

  pp [signature here]

  Trevor Jones,
  Marketing Director

* If 'pp' is taken to stand for Latin *per pro* ('for and on behalf of'), then it should precede the name of the person who dictated the letter:

  . . . . . .

  Yours sincerely,

  [signature here]
  pp Trevor Jones

  Marketing Director

In practice, the second version is now the more common of the two, but both are correct. In either case, your reply should always be addressed to the person who dictated the letter (in this example, Trevor Jones), not the person who signed it.

Business-letter style

Make your letter as short as possible; strictly to the point; sufficiently (but not excessively) detailed; accurate; and courteous. **Say what you have to say, say it clearly, and say nothing more** (apart from the normal courtesies).

The language of a business letter, while of course formal rather than informal, should not be very different from your everyday language. Avoid stilted and unnatural English: there is no need to use words like 'commence' or 'deem' when you would more naturally say 'begin' or 'think'. And definitely avoid old-fashioned commercialese such as 'I beg to inform you . . .' ('I am writing to inform you . . .' would be better) or 'Please find enclosed . . .' ('I enclose . . .' would be preferable).

If you are writing on behalf of a company or organisation, say 'we', 'us' and 'our'; if you are writing in a personal capacity, write 'I', 'me' and 'my'.

Abbreviations

Contrary to what many people think, abbreviations are not a necessary or even desirable part of business letters. Write 'account' rather than 'a/c', 'approximately' rather than 'approx.', 'attention' rather than 'attn.', and so on. Do not use technical abbreviations that the person reading your letter might not be familiar with, such as 'OOS' for 'out of stock'. Similarly, do not use the once-standard abbreviations 'inst.' for 'of this month', 'prox.' for 'of next month' or 'ult.' for 'of last month' in dates. (You can, of course, still use normal everyday abbreviations such as 'e.g.' or 'i.e.')

Structure

There will be three parts to the main text of your letter:

- an introductory paragraph outlining the subject or purpose of the letter;

- one or more paragraphs in which you develop what you have to say;

- a concluding paragraph to round the letter off.

Introductory paragraph

The introductory paragraph may consist of no more than one sentence. It will refer to and expand slightly on the heading, so that the subject of the letter is clear. In it you will refer to any previous correspondence, or perhaps to a telephone conversation that the letter is a follow-up to.

Previous contact details

It is always wise when telephoning on business to make a note of the date and time, and of the name of the person you are speaking to, so that you can refer to them in any follow-up letter (e.g. 'Further to my telephone conversation with Miss Eagleton this morning, I am writing to confirm . . .').

Development

The main body of the letter develops your topic. You list facts, you give explanations, you put forward proposals, and so on.

If you have a lot to say in this part of your letter, you may find when you have drafted it that the paragraphs are too long or complicated and that what you are saying is hard to follow. Rewrite the letter with shorter and clearer paragraphs. (Each paragraph should only cover one topic or make one main point.) You might use bullet points or numbered paragraphs, or even give your paragraphs short headings. Consider whether anything needs to be reordered to make a more logical argument. (Look again at the writing and checking process outlined in Chapter 5.) The key thing is that the person who receives and reads your letter should be able to grasp what you have written without having to reread it several times.

If you are copying your letter to someone else, you can indicate this by adding a 'cc' note at the end of the letter after the complimentary close:

cc Angus Argyll, Kim Hunter

This is fine if the main recipient knows who Angus Argyll and Kim Hunter are, but it may be mystifying (and rather discourteous) to a recipient who does not, and therefore has no idea why these people have been sent a copy of the correspondence. In such cases it is better to state at the end of the development section of your letter who you are copying the letter to and who exactly they are:

I am sending a copy of this letter to Angus Argyll, our Marketing Director, and to Kim Hunter, our Sales Manager.

If you are enclosing one or more documents with your letter, you should list them in your letter so that nothing goes astray (or if something does, there is a clear record of it having been sent with the letter). As with 'cc', you can write 'Encl.' or 'Encs' (for 'Enclosures') at the foot of your letter, followed by whatever documents you have enclosed:

Encl.: Notarised copy of birth certificate

Alternatively, you can state in the body of the letter what document(s) you are enclosing:

I enclose a notarised copy of my birth certificate.

> There is no point in putting 'Encs' at the end of a letter unless you make it clear what the enclosures are: if something is mislaid, how is anyone to know what they are looking for?

Concluding paragraph

Your letter should end with a short paragraph containing some expression of goodwill or thanks, an expression of hope that the recipient is satisfied with your letter, an assurance of your willingness to deal with any further queries, problems or complaints, and so on (whatever is appropriate in the context).

Continuation sheets

If the letter you are writing requires more than one sheet of paper and you use headed notepaper for the first sheet, the second and any subsequent sheets should be plain paper; only the first sheet should be headed. The pages should be numbered, and it is often recommended that the addressee and the date should be typed in the top left-hand corner of each sheet:

2/
Bognor Brothers plc
19 October 2010

Covering letters

If you are sending documents, do not simply put them in an envelope and send them off. Even if you have been asked for the documents, it is wise to accompany them with a covering letter making clear for whom the documents are intended and for what purpose. In a large office, for example in the civil service, the person who deals with your letter may not be the person who has asked to see the documents and may not know the background.

As with any other business letter, make sure the covering letter is dated, has a topic line, and has any relevant reference numbers. List each of the documents enclosed; this may be helpful if in the future you want to confirm what was sent and when.

Dear Mrs Armitage,

Death of Mrs Joanne Seymour

Thank you for your very helpful telephone conversation yesterday afternoon regarding the death of my wife and what is required to make a claim on her life insurance policy.

As requested, I enclose the following documents:

- *insurance policy MSD/109865/JS*
- *a notarised copy of my wife's birth certificate*
- *a notarised copy of my wife's death certificate*

Thank you for your assistance with this claim, and also for your kind words to me yesterday.

Yours sincerely, ...

Copies of letters

Always keep a copy of any letter you send. You may want to refer to it at some later time, and it may be important to know exactly what was said (or sent). And of course, keep all letters that you receive as well, as they too may be required for future reference.

Varieties of business letters

There are, of course, as many varieties of business letters as there are different business situations and topics. Only a small sample can be included in this book, but they should nevertheless be sufficient to indicate the principles that apply in any situation. Some have already been looked at; a few more follow below.

Booking accommodation

Hotel reservations can very often be made on the internet now, but for those who don't have this facility, a letter may be required to follow up and confirm a telephone booking.

You need to confirm every key aspect of the arrangements: the day of your arrival and how long you are staying, how many adults and children, the number and type of rooms booked, the agreed cost, etc. Mention any extras or particular requirements that have been agreed, such as a children's cot or special dietary needs. Especially if you are booking into a small hotel, guest house or B & B, it would also be courteous to let the owner know at what time you expect to arrive, and to say that you will telephone them should there be any change to your plans. The following letter covers all these points:

The Goose Inn
St Cyril Street
Stambourne
MQ4 3ET

Dear Sirs,

Confirmation of accommodation booking

Further to my telephone call earlier this evening, I am writing to confirm the booking of a double room for two adults and a twin-bedded room for two children, both rooms with en-suite bath-rooms, for bed and breakfast for the nights of Friday 27 August and Saturday 28 August.

I understand the total cost of this will be £240. As requested, I enclose a non-returnable deposit of £60.

As I informed your receptionist this evening, we will be bringing our pet spaniel with us, and I would be glad if you would confirm that it is acceptable for us to have her with us in our room. She has frequently been with us in hotels, and has never created any prob-lems for staff or other guests in the past.

We expect to arrive at the hotel about 8 o'clock, and will telephone you should there be any significant change to these plans.

I would be glad to receive confirmation of this booking at your earliest convenience.

With thanks,

Yours faithfully, ...

Ordering a product

As with booking accommodation, theatre tickets, and so on, ordering goods can often be done online or by telephone, or you may simply need to fill in details of the goods you want on a pre-printed order form. However, there may be occasions when you need to place an order by letter, in which case the following rules apply:

- Specify the product you want by name, and also give the company's product reference number if it has one.

- Give any other relevant descriptive details (size, colour, etc).

- Clearly specify the address to which the goods are to be delivered, and any other relevant arrangements such as time of delivery.

- State your intended method of payment, and whether payment is enclosed or will be made on delivery of the goods.

The following letter is an example that could easily be adapted for other products or situations:

44 Barland Avenue
Marfield
SX7 9KT
Tel. 01689 740 674

10 Feb 2010

Jardinaids Ltd
Wentworth Close
Lomanby
CX2 6YH

Dear Sirs,

Wonderwheels Gardener's Barrow

I saw an advertisement for your Wonderwheels Gardener's Barrow in this weekend's Marfield Post, and I would like to order one from you.

I understand the barrow is available in three sizes and several colours. The model I would like is the medium-size, dark-blue version (your catalogue reference WGB-2-db). However, if you do not have this model in stock at the moment, the equivalent dark-green version (WGB-2-dg) would be quite acceptable.

I enclose a cheque for £33.95 to cover the cost and delivery of the barrow.

Please deliver the barrow to the address at the top of this letter. I understand I can expect delivery within 7 working days. I shall telephone you in a few days' time to confirm when the barrow is likely to arrive so that I can make any necessary arrangements for taking delivery of it.

With thanks,

Yours faithfully, ...

Advertising flyers and letters

If you are trying to advertise your services, for example by putting information about your business through the letter boxes of potential customers, a flyer is often much better than a letter. Most people receive a great deal of junk mail which they have absolutely no interest in reading, and therefore you need something that will attract their attention and get your key selling-points across in the time it takes them to walk from the front door to the rubbish bin. No matter how well written – and the more you write, the more likely you are to make mistakes – an advert in the form of a letter may simply look boring. A bright and well-illustrated flyer, with only key points highlighted, is much more likely to get the householder's attention.

Even a flyer should not have too much text on it. Among the key points that need to stand out immediately might be:

- the range of services you offer

- your experience, reliability and affordability

- that your work is guaranteed

- where and how you can be contacted

- how quickly you will respond

- that you offer free estimates

Write down all the selling-points you want to include, think how you would like the flyer to be illustrated, and then go and talk to a printer.

Nevertheless, there may be times when a letter is more appropriate than a flyer. If you are writing to someone you know is a potential customer and will probably be interested in your product or services, your letter can be longer and more informative, because you can assume you have their attention as soon as they have opened it. For example, many firms in the building, decorating and furnishing trades regularly check planning applications for house extensions or conservatories, and target their mailings accordingly.

Here is an example of an advertising letter:

Dear Mr and Mrs Adam,

We have noted from the planning application you have recently submitted to the local Planning Department that you are intending to build a conservatory.

We are a building company that has specialised in the construction of house extensions, roof extensions and conservatories for more than 20 years.

We can offer you a prompt, reliable, efficient and personal service and workmanship of the highest quality, all at a very competitive price.

We have enclosed a leaflet showing some of the standard conservatories we offer, but we can also provide a personalized design service to create for you a unique conservatory tailored to your exact specifications.

For more information, and a free, no-obligation quotation, please contact our sales manager, Jim Forsyth, on 01357 864208.

We look forward to hearing from you.

Yours sincerely, ...

Key points to note

- If you have the householder's name, address them by name. 'Dear Sir or Madam' suggests that you are not really very interested in them as individuals, that this is just a circular letter sent out without much thought or attention.

- Make your sentences and paragraphs short and snappy.

- Key words can be highlighted to make them stand out (but don't get carried away).

- Check your spelling, grammar and punctuation. If you know this is not your strong point, get someone reliable to check it.

- Offer your services but don't grovel.

Quotation for work

A quotation for work requires a detailed statement of work, materials and estimated costs:

- It should be written on headed notepaper, including your full business address, email address (if you have one), and daytime and evening telephone numbers (including your mobile phone number, if you have one, so that potential customers can contact you while you are at work). If you do not have headed notepaper, the above information should be given in full at the top of your letter.

- Give the name and address of your potential customer.

- Date the quotation.

- Describe exactly the work to be carried out; make an itemised list if necessary.

- State the quantity and precise names, colours, etc of the products being supplied (include product code numbers if this might be helpful).

- State clearly the dates and/or timescale for the work to be carried out.

- State the length of any guarantee.

- State how long your quotation holds good for, and whether written confirmation of acceptance of the quotation is required.

- State whether a deposit is necessary before work begins.

DOMBEY ROOFING LTD
23 London Road
Sunbury SN7 0QT
Tel: 01383 674321 Mob: 07797 642874

10.9.10

Mr Smith
17 Mountjoy Park
Sunbury

ESTIMATE: REFELTING OF FRONT PORCH ROOF

- *Strip off defective covering and remove from site.*

- *Inspect wooden boarding under felt and consult with owner on findings.*

- *Prepare boarding for the application of roofing felt.*

- *Apply three layers of roofing felt:*

  - *First layer to consist of reinforced underlay*

  - *Second layer to consist of 2mm polyester-based felt*

  - *Top layer to consist of 4mm polyester-based felt.*

- *All layers to be well lapped and secured by galvanised tacks and/or fusion.*

The top layer of felt carries a manufacturers' ten-year guarantee.

The work should be completed within one working day.

Costs: materials £107; labour £140.
Total cost (apart from the cost of any work that may need to be carried out on boarding): £247 including VAT.

This quotation remains valid for six months. Please confirm acceptance in writing. A 10% deposit is required before the work is started.

We hope this quotation meets with your approval. Should you require further information, please contact Mr H Dombey.

Accepting a quotation

When accepting a quotation, it is not necessary to repeat all the details that have been set out in it. Both you and the contractor have them already in the quotation. However, if there are any details that have not been included (such as paint colours or wallpaper patterns), you should clearly state these in your letter of acceptance. No work should begin until both parties have a copy in writing of all the details that need to be agreed. It is not a question of dishonesty, but misunderstandings can occur and memories can play tricks. If everything is in writing, both parties know exactly what is expected.

Make sure also that you understand any technical terms used by the contractor in the quotation. (Do you know what a 'soffit' is, and do you actually want it to be painted?)

Confirm the date(s) by which payment(s) will be made.

If you require any alteration or addition to what has been set out in the quotation, contact the contractor by letter detailing the changes that need to be made. And of course keep a copy of the letter for yourself.

Tel: 01383 315684

17 Mountjoy Park
Sunbury
SN3 0TK

14 Sept 2010

Dombey Roofing Ltd
23 London Road
Sunbury SN7 0QT

Dear Sirs,

REFELTING OF FRONT PORCH ROOF, 17 MOUNTJOY PARK

Thank you for your quotation, dated 10 September, for the above job.

I confirm that your outline of the work to be carried out is acceptable, as is the price you quote.

I agree that any work needing to be done on the boarding under the felt is not included in the price quoted, and will require to be agreed between us at the time the work is carried out.

I enclose a cheque for £24.70 as the requested deposit, and will pay the rest of the costs by cheque on satisfactory completion of the work.

Please telephone me at your earliest convenience to agree a suitable date for the work to be carried out.

With thanks,

Yours faithfully, ...

Faxes

There is little to say about faxing except that a faxed document should always be accompanied by a cover sheet stating who the fax is meant for, the sender's details, the number of pages being sent, and whether or not it is confidential (though faxing may not always be a wise way of sending a confidential document, as you do not know who might see it at the receiving end).

This information should be stated as succinctly as possible. Since the covering note is not itself a letter, there is no need for the salutation and complimentary close that would be expected in a letter. If the document does not include your phone and fax numbers, these should be given on the cover sheet. If copies are being sent to someone else, this should be indicated.

A fax cover sheet could be laid out as follows:

FAX

To:
From:
Phone: *Fax:*
Date:
Subject:
Pages:

Some useful phrases

- I refer to your letter of 23 June.

- Thank you for your letter dated 23 June 2010.

- I refer to my telephone conversation with . . . this afternoon.

- Further to my telephone call this morning, . . .

- I apologise sincerely for . . .

- Please accept our sincere apologies for . . .

- I am very sorry for the inconvenience this has caused you.

- I would appreciate confirmation of the delivery date.

- Could you please confirm when I can expect . . . to be delivered.

- There are several points in your letter which are not entirely clear.

- I would appreciate the opportunity to discuss this matter with you further.

- I look forward to hearing from you soon.

- I look forward to your response.

- I look forward to hearing from you and wish to thank you again for your assistance with this matter.

- Assuring you of our best attention at all times, . . .

- Thank you once again for your assistance.

- Thank you for your co-operation in this matter.

- Thank you in advance for your anticipated co-operation in this matter.

Memos

Memos are short business communications, generally between colleagues within an office or organisation.

A business or organisation usually has its own standard printed memo forms, but if you are creating your own the following format applies. A memo comes in two sections, one above the other:

- The top section should state who the memo is being sent to, who it is from, whether it is being copied to anyone else, the date (and possibly the time) it is being sent, and the subject, all laid out in much the same way as the cover sheet for a fax. You can use initials to identify yourself, the recipient(s) of the memo, and anyone you are copying the memo to, so long as it is clear who is who.

- The bottom section is for the message itself. Memos should be as short as possible, without being cryptic or unintelligible. No salutation or complimentary close is necessary, just the text of the message, as in the following example.

MEMO

To: AHD, RCF, LC
From: JG
CC: MT
Date/time: Monday 25 Oct
Subject: Sales forecasts

Can I remind you all that I need your area sales forecasts for the period January–July 2011 by the end of this week. Thanks.

12 Complaints, criticisms and apologies

There is, apparently, an old Chinese proverb that says: 'Never write a letter when you are angry.' Actually, there is a lot to be said for writing a letter when you are angry: it lets you say all the things you really want to say just when you want to say them. It doesn't matter if what you say is justified (or even true), it doesn't matter if what you say would make you curl up in embarrassment at any other time; if it makes you feel better, get it all off your chest and down on paper. There is, however, one important thing to remember: when you have written your letter,

DO NOT SEND IT!

It has served its purpose. Now tear it up.

For at least a couple of hours, ignore whatever it is that has provoked your wrath. Think about something else. Deal with something else. Do something else. Better still, sleep on it. The letter can wait, and it will be much better for you and everyone else concerned if it does.

For this reason, a letter is much safer than an email: with an email, only the 'Send' button stands between you and the consequences of an over-hasty reaction, whereas with a letter, you need paper, a pen, an

---

Never write, or reply to, a letter of complaint or criticism until you have got the issues into perspective and your anger under control.

envelope, a stamp, and a walk to the postbox – which gives you plenty of time to reconsider what you are doing.

The form of a letter of complaint

A letter of complaint may be written in either the indented or the blocked style (see Chapter 1). A letter of complaint from a business would normally be written in the blocked style of a business letter, whereas a personal letter of complaint might well be written in the less formal indented style.

Key points for letters of complaint or criticism

- Be sure that you have a valid cause for complaint.

- Be sure that you are complaining to the right person/people.

- Be sure to explain clearly the exact nature of your complaint.

- Be clear (in your own mind and in your letter) about what you are asking the recipient of the letter to do with regard to your complaint. Are you asking for an apology, for compensation for some loss or inconvenience (or simply an assurance that whatever has happened will not happen again), for a replacement or refund for faulty goods, etc?

- Remember that the most effective communication is one that keeps to facts and does not cast pointless and perhaps unjustified aspersions. Do not assume what you do not know. Do not impute motives you cannot possibly be sure of.

- Don't try to impress with big words and pompous phrases. A simple and straightforward statement of the facts is what is required.

- Remember that being abusive is counterproductive. No matter how much you think someone is at fault, if you want their help, making them feel bad or angry is not likely to enlist it.

- Do not threaten action that you have no intention of carrying out or that would be against the law. You may not like your neighbour's 60 ft leylandii hedge or what their cat does in your garden, but the law clearly defines what action you can take with regard to them.

- Always assume that the person you are writing to will be willing to recognise their mistake and to rectify it if they can. They may not have intended what they did – or what you think they did. We are all human; honest mistakes happen.

- Remember that the company/person you are writing to may not be at fault. (If, for example, something you have ordered from a business does not arrive, that doesn't mean that it wasn't dispatched.) In the first instance, a polite enquiry may be more appropriate than a complaint.

- Even when making a complaint, it may be possible to find something to praise as well. If so, do so. (For example: 'While I must compliment you on your prompt service, I am afraid the goods you have sent me are faulty.') This may get the recipient of the letter into a good frame of mind to deal equally promptly with your complaint.

Complaints about goods and services

In addition to the above points, there are a number of things to remember specifically when complaining to a business about goods and services:

- Remember that the person who reads your letter may not be the person responsible for the situation you are complaining about.

- If you do not know who to write to, address your complaint to the Customer Complaints Department or the Customer Services Manager. Even if no such department or manager exists, this will nevertheless make the nature of your letter clear and ensure that it quickly reaches the person whose job it is to deal with customer complaints. For smaller firms, address your letter to the owner or managing director.

- Give your letter a heading, which should include details such as the order number, product number or model, and your receipt, invoice or guarantee number.

- Give full details of the problem, explaining why you are dissatisfied. Make sure you put down all the relevant facts.

- If you have previously spoken to someone on the telephone, give the date and time of the call, the name of the person you spoke to, and what was said.

- As mentioned above, you must state clearly what you would like to be done about the problem: do you want a replacement, a refund or just an apology? If you are going to hold the company to the terms of their guarantee, you should state this. (Make sure you make a claim for compensation or refund within any time limit stated in the guarantee.) If you are sure of your rights under consumer legislation, you might mention these as well.

- If you include relevant documents, such as guarantees or receipts, send copies. Never send the originals, in case they get mislaid.

- It may be wise to state a date by which you expect to receive a reply to your letter. This gives you a reason to contact the firm again if you do not receive a reply within the time limit you have set.

- If you do not receive a satisfactory reply, write again, stating (in a polite, non-threatening manner) any further action you intend to take.

- It is a good idea to send your letter by recorded delivery, which means there will be a record of its having been delivered.

- Keep copies of all letters you send.

Some useful phrases

- I wish to complain about . . .

- I am writing to complain about . . .

- I am writing to make a complaint about . . .

- I wish to express my dissatisfaction regarding . . .

- I am writing to inform you of our dissatisfaction with . . .

- I am sorry to have to say that I was not entirely satisfied with . . .

- My main complaint is that . . .

- I enclose a list of my complaints.

- I wish to draw your attention to . . .

- I find it totally unsatisfactory that . . .

- The service we were offered was unsatisfactory in the following ways: . . .

- When I unpacked the . . . , I found the following defects/ damage: . . .

- When I tried to assemble the . . . , I experienced the following problems/found the following parts were missing: . . .

- I do not wish to blame any of your staff for what happened, but . . .

- Of course I realise that mistakes do happen from time to time, but . . .

- I'm sure this is a rare problem, but . . .

- I realise that this is an uncharacteristic lapse in your normally excellent customer service, but . . .

- Your quotation quite clearly stated/included . . .

- In terms of the contract between us, I expected . . .

- Under the terms of the guarantee, . . .

- I would appreciate/be grateful for your help in resolving this matter.

- I look forward to a speedy resolution of this problem.

- I look forward to hearing from you.

- I look forward to hearing from you at your earliest convenience.

- I look forward to your suggestions as to how this matter can be put right.

- I look forward to receiving your reply within the next . . . days.

- I would be interested in any comments you might care to make regarding . . .

- I would be grateful if you would send me a replacement.

- Please telephone me to let me know how you intend to deal with this matter.

- Could I please ask you to look into this matter.

- Can I ask that you look into this as a matter of urgency.

- I look forward to receiving your explanation for . . .

- If I am not satisfied by your response, I may be forced to take legal action.

- If I am still not satisfied, I may refer this matter to my solicitor/the small claims court.

One example of a letter of complaint can be seen on page 11. The following pages contain some others.

The Customer Service Manager
Blue & Black Buses
Dockenby
NC8 7GH

Dear Sir or Madam,

<u>Service 35 Dockenby to Norton Spencely</u>

I would like to draw your attention to a problem that frequently occurs with the No. 35 buses as they pass along Fenny Road in the direction of Norton Spencely, especially during the morning rush hour.

There is a bus stop about halfway along Fenny Road, more or less opposite the Grove Garage, at which Service 35 buses are supposed to stop. It would appear, however, that some of your drivers are either unaware of this bus stop or for some reason choose to ignore it, driving past on the outside lane even though the buses are not full and there are passengers at the bus stop clearly signalling their wish to get on.

I would be grateful if you could remind your drivers on this route that this bus stop exists and that they should be prepared to stop at it if requested to do so.

I look forward to seeing a marked improvement in this service within the next few days.

Thank you for your assistance.

Yours faithfully, ...

Notice that in the above letter, the first paragraph introduces the issue, the second paragraph outlines more fully the reason for the complaint, the third paragraph states what action should be taken by the recipient of the letter, and the fourth paragraph states what the result of this action should be. A similar structure can be seen in the following letter, with the addition of a final paragraph stating the action the letter-writer will take if the matter is not satisfactorily resolved:

The Customer Complaints Department,
John Gower & Sons (Electrical) Ltd,
20 Milton Lane,
Lanefield

Dear Sirs,

Arctic Dishwasher AR1089
Purchased 11 Sept 2010, Receipt No. 108947

My husband and I recently bought an Arctic dishwasher from your shop. It was installed by your company's own service engineers on Wednesday 15 September.

The dishwasher ran without any problems for about two weeks but then we noticed a damp patch in the carpet round the machine and realised that water was leaking out from under it every time we used it. We have therefore stopped running the dishwasher for the time being.

I telephoned your Customer Service Department last Monday morning (4 October), and spoke to Jane Freeman. She said she would arrange for a service engineer to call round to examine the machine on Wednesday morning. I took the morning off work in order to be at home when the engineer called, but no one came.

I telephoned again that afternoon, and spoke to Susan, Jane Freeman apparently not being available at that time. She could not explain why no one had called that morning, but assured me that an engineer would definitely call round this afternoon (Thursday 7 Oct). I was in the house for the whole afternoon, and yet again your service engineer failed to appear.

My husband and I are therefore faced with the double inconvenience of having no working dishwasher for the time being, and the need for one or other of us to take yet another morning or afternoon off work in order for it to be repaired. This is really quite unsatisfactory, and not the level of service I expect from a company of your standing.

I would be grateful if someone from your department would telephone me at the beginning of next week (at my office phone number given at the top of this letter) and give me a definite day and time when a service engineer will call and repair the dishwasher.

If this matter is not resolved by the end of next week at the latest, my husband and I will have no option but to employ a firm of domestic appliance engineers to carry out the repair work and recover the costs from you. I hope this will not be necessary.

Yours faithfully, ...

Apologies

The situations requiring apologies are as varied as the situations that give rise to complaints. Everyone makes mistakes, and there is bound to be some time in your life when you have to apologise for something. You may be apologising for something you have said or done, or you may be responding to a complaint or criticism you have received. You may be apologising for something that you are personally responsible for, or you may be apologising on behalf of someone else, such as a company or organisation. The letters will be different but the basic principles are much the same in all cases.

If you are responding to a letter of complaint, reply by letter; an email might cause further offence. If, on the other hand, you have received a complaint by email, you can assume that the writer considers email appropriate for correspondence of this sort and will not be offended by an emailed reply (and indeed might be angered by anything other than the immediate response that email allows). In other circumstances, only you can decide whether an email would be acceptable or whether a letter would be more suitable. But if in doubt, err on the safe side and be conventional: a letter will not offend, whereas an email might.

Key points for letters of apology

- Write your apology as soon as possible after the offence occurs or the complaint is received. Even if you do not have enough information to fully address a complaint immediately, you should respond at once, so that the complainer knows that their complaint has been received and the matter is receiving attention.

- If for some reason you cannot write immediately, apologise for the delay when you do write.

- If writing on behalf of a company or organisation, it is correct to use 'we'; if writing in your own capacity on behalf of a company or organisation, use 'I'.

- If responding to a complaint, thank the person for getting in touch with you. In a business context, you can say that you value customers' feedback, as it allows you to improve your service.

- Keep your apology short, simple, sincere and to the point. There is no need to go on and on about how bad you feel; just say sorry.

- If possible, give a reason for what happened.

- No matter how rude or angry the complainer is, no matter how foolish or unjustified you may consider their complaint to be, your response should be polite and (as far as possible) conciliatory. Your aim should be to dampen the flames of outrage, not fan them into something worse.

- A letter of complaint may include a number of separate points. Make sure that you address them all, or else you may seem not to be taking the complaint seriously enough. If necessary, set them out in separate paragraphs or as a series of bullet points. Once you have written your reply, check that you have covered everything.

- Not all letters of complaint will be written in perfect and coherent English. It is up to you to decipher every letter as best you can, and to address with all seriousness the points the writer seems to be making.

- Take responsibility for what has happened; apologise for the inconvenience, embarrassment or hurt caused; and say what you will do to rectify the situation (if that is possible – it may not always be).

- If possible and appropriate, give assurances that the mistake or misdemeanour will not happen again in the future.

The following sample letters of apology can be adapted to fit a number of situations:

Dear Belinda,

When I got back home from this evening's meeting, my face was still burning with shame.

I don't know what got into me this evening. Even though I disagree with you about how we should spend the money we raised at the flower show, I had no reason, and no right, to speak to you the way I did. And in front of other people too!

I have always been a bit quick-tempered – you've probably noticed that before. Most people have! – and it is a side of my personality that I find both infuriating and embarrassing. I do try not to let my tongue get the better of me, but there are times when the words are out before I can catch myself, and tonight was one of those times.

Of course I apologised at once to you, and you were very gracious about the whole thing, but I wanted to write and apologise again. I hope you really can forgive me. I would hate what happened this evening to spoil a friendship that I have valued for so many years.

Yours,
Jane

The Secretary,
Bannockmore Burns Club,
11 Avon Road,
Bannockmore

29 November 2010

Dear Mr Maclean,

I have been very much looking forward to addressing the Bannockmore Burns Club at your Burns Supper in January, and I would like to thank you again for inviting me to propose the Immortal Memory.

Unfortunately, because of work commitments I had not foreseen, I find that I will have to be in China at that time, and will therefore not be able to speak at the Supper as planned.

I do apologise for this. I realise that it may cause you some inconvenience to find yourselves without a speaker at this late date, and if I could alter my arrangements to suit both you and my employers, I would.

If it would be of any help to you, my brother-in-law, Phil Brown, would probably be willing to come to your Burns Supper in my place. He is an experienced speaker and has given the speech to the Immortal Memory at several Burns Suppers in the past, but has as yet no commitments for next January. Do let me know if you would like me to approach him.

With my sincere apologies again for having to let you down,

Yours sincerely,

[signature here]

Ronald Mack

Mr T Sheridan
23 Rosewood Gardens
Romerton
PM10 3RS

16 September 2010

Dear Mr Sheridan,

Order Number 10/67153

Thank you for your letter of 14 September, in which you explain to us the difficulty you have experienced in attempting to use our own-brand Anis toner cartridges in your Takto printer.

I am sorry that you have experienced a problem for which I can at present offer no explanation. We have never had such a problem brought to our attention before, and we have many satisfied customers who regularly use our Anis toner cartridges in their Takto printers.

It may be that there is some fault in the particular cartridges you have been sent and we would therefore be glad if you would return them to us for examination so that we can establish whether this is the case. We enclose a stamped, addressed mailing bag for this purpose.

When our technical staff have established the nature of the problem, I will be in contact with you again. In the meantime, I have pleasure in enclosing two Takto toner cartridges as a replacement *for the Anis cartridges you have been unable to use.*

With apologies again for the inconvenience this has caused you,

Yours sincerely,

[**signature here**]

Adam Brett
Customer Services Manager

Some useful phrases

- I was concerned to learn that . . .

- We were most concerned to receive your letter of . . . regarding . . .

- I apologise for . . .

- I would like to apologise for . . .

- I am very sorry that . . .

- We are very sorry that the . . . you received was defective.

- Please accept my sincere apologies for . . .

- I apologise for any annoyance/inconvenience that this may have caused you.

- I would like to apologise for any inconvenience this has caused.

- I appreciate that this must be extremely frustrating.

- I appreciate how inconvenient this must be for you, and . . .

- We appreciate the inconvenience this must have caused you.

- We apologise for whatever inconvenience this may cause you, but . . .

- We accept full responsibility for what happened.

- I am pleased to be able to inform you that . . .

- There is no question that the . . . you received did not meet the high standards our customers have come to expect.

- We will put things right at the earliest opportunity.

- To compensate for the inconvenience this has caused you, we would like to . . .

- We are enclosing . . . with our compliments.

- We are happy to offer you a full refund for . . .

- I am sorry I am unable to answer your question immediately.

- If you have any questions, please contact . . .

- I hope that you will have no further cause for complaint with regard to our service.

- Thank you for your patience/co-operation/understanding.

- Thank you for bringing this matter to our attention.

- Your feedback/comments will prove invaluable to us as we seek to improve our service.

13 Letters relating to employment

Job applications

The purpose of a job application is not so much to get you a job as to get you an interview with the person who can offer you a job. (What happens at the interview itself is beyond the scope of this book. For that, you should read *Perfect Interview* and *Perfect Answers to Interview Questions*, in the same series.) The main problem you have to overcome is that you are likely to be just one of many applicants, and your potential employer has no particular reason to look with greater interest or favour at your application than at any other. The purpose of your application, therefore, is to give them a good reason to want to interview you. (The other side of the coin is that it must also give them no reason to decide *not* to interview you.) Your application must make an immediate good impression on someone who may spend no more than a few minutes – if even that long – skimming through it before picking up the next one in the pile.

Application scenarios

There are two main types of application for employment:

- an application in response to a job advertisement, and

- a speculative approach to a company or organisation.

Do not imagine that the second approach is a waste of time: it has been estimated that over 80% of jobs are never advertised. If you approach a company with a convincing reason for them to employ you, it saves them the time, trouble and expense of looking for you (or someone else).

CVs and covering letters

A job application generally consists of two parts: a curriculum vitae (CV) and a covering letter. Broadly speaking, the CV gives a detailed overview of your education, skills and experience (along with your personal details), while the covering letter highlights the key points you want to pick out in the hope of arousing the interest of the person reading it.

The covering letter

It is the covering letter that a potential employer will read first, so it is crucial that it makes a favourable impression:

- Your letter should be clear, neat, concise and to the point. Remember that it does not have to, indeed should not, repeat all the information you will have included in your CV.

- Type your letter unless the advert specifies (as some do) that it should be handwritten. Use black ink, and white paper. If keying, use an easy-to-read typeface in 11- or 12-point, and set wide margins. A4 would be a sensible size of paper. (Of course, nowadays you may be asked to send your CV and covering letter by email. For the email format of a letter, see Chapter 4.)

- Your letter should ideally be no more than one page in length.

- Your letter should have no corrections on it. If you make a mistake, redo the whole letter.

- Like any other letter, your covering letter should be 'topped and tailed' in the usual way: your address, email address and telephone number; date; the name, title and address of the person you are writing to; appropriate salutation; appropriate complimentary close. (Check Chapter 1 again if there is anything here you are not sure about.)

- If you normally use a rather quaint or zany email address, you might do well to consider giving yourself a more straightforward one for the purposes of job applications.

- Do not address your letter to someone solely by their title (such as 'The Personnel Manager' or 'The Director of Human Resources'). Take the trouble to find out the name of the person you will be sending your application to (e.g. by checking the website of the company or organisation, or even simply by calling up the company/organisation and asking the receptionist), and refer to them by both name and title in your letter:

Mrs Joan Seaton
Personnel Manager
. . . . . .

Dear Mrs Seaton,
. . . . . .

- If you are applying for more than one job, do not use the same covering letter every time. There may be slight differences in the approach you should take with each application, so take the time to reconsider and alter your letter where necessary.

- Begin the letter with a heading indicating the post you are applying for, including (if you are responding to an advert) any reference number. The first paragraph should briefly expand on this:

Dear Mrs Seaton,

Area Sales Executive, SW England

I am writing in response to your company's advertisement in the Daily Post of 22 September for an Area Sales Executive for the south-west of England.

- As shown above, if you are responding to an advertisement, it is normal to say where you saw the job advertised.

- The second and subsequent paragraphs should develop your application, explaining your interest in the post or in the company/organisation, highlighting your qualifications, skills and experience, and outlining why you think you would be suitable for the job. If the advertisement specifies any particular requirements, be sure to show that you meet them. In a nutshell, you remind the company what they are looking for (based on what the advert stipulates) and you outline why you are the ideal person for the job.

> Take care to focus on what you can do for the company/organisation, not on what you would hope to get out of the job. And try not to begin every paragraph with 'I'.

- If there is a way to show that you have some knowledge of the company/organisation, fit this in too. It would certainly be wise to do some 'homework' before writing your application. If there is something that the company/organisation claims for itself (e.g. that it has a strong commitment to environmental responsibility, or that it is a leader in the field of paint technology), respond to this in a positive way.

- If you are writing 'on spec' to a company/organisation, say where you heard about them, mention something good that you know about them, and say what has attracted you to them and why you are applying for a position with them. If someone has told you about an employment opportunity, say so and (if they do not object) name them:

Dear Mrs Seaton,

Stock controller

*My sister-in-law, Betty Hamilton, who works in your accounts
department, has told me that your company may have a vacancy
for a stock controller.*

- Mention that you are enclosing your CV with your letter.

- Your final paragraph should indicate your availability for an
  interview.

Here are two examples of covering letters showing the different
approaches in the context of the same job:

Letter in response to a job advertisement

Email: mcanmore29@anisp.co.uk   *7 Nonesuch Hill*
Tel: 01479 846200   *Delmartin*
                                         Lincs
                                         DL3 9FR

                                         23 October 2010

Mrs Joan Seaton
Personnel Manager
Helergen Solar Panels plc
Letford Industrial Estate
Letford
MX15 7QI

Dear Mrs Seaton,

Area Sales Manager, SW England; reference 10/09ASE

I am writing in response to your company's advertisement in the *Daily Post* of 22 September for an Area Sales Manager for the south-west of England.

At present I am a senior sales executive with seven years' experience in plumbing and electrical supplies, operating in the south of England for a major wholesale company. Over the past four years, I have trebled my sales figures, and have twice won my present employers' Sales Representative of the Year Award.

I was very pleased to see this vacancy advertised, as I am keen to move into the field of renewable energy, both because I see it as a growing market and also because I have a strong commitment to environmentalism and would very much like to use my sales experience and expertise to promote the use of environmentally-friendly sources of energy such as yours. I am willing to travel as part of my job.

I would welcome the opportunity to discuss with you the contribution I could make to the future growth and development of Helergen Solar Panels.

My CV is enclosed, and I would be happy to provide you with any further information you require.

I look forward to hearing from you.

Yours sincerely,

[signature here]

Malcolm Canmore

Speculative approach to a company or organisation

Email: mcanmore29@anisp.co.uk

Tel: 01479 846200

7 Nonesuch Hill

Delmartin

Lincs

DL3 9FR

23 October 2010

Mrs Joan Seaton

Personnel Manager

Helergen Solar Panels plc

Letford Industrial Estate

Letford

MX15 7QI

Dear Mrs Seaton,

I was very interested to read the article about Helergen Solar Panels plc in last Saturday's Daily Post. I recognise Helergen as one of the leaders in the field of solar energy, and it is for this reason that I am writing to you to inquire whether there might be a position for me in your company.

At present I am a senior sales executive with seven years' experience in plumbing and electrical supplies, operating in the south of England for a major wholesale company. Over the past four years, I have trebled my sales figures, and have twice won my present employers' Sales Representative of the Year Award.

I am very keen to move into the field of renewable energy, both because I see it as a growing market and also because I have a strong commitment to environmentalism and would very much like to use my sales experience and expertise to promote the use of *environmentally-friendly sources of energy such as yours. I am willing to travel as part of my job.*

I would welcome an opportunity to discuss with you the contribution I could make to the future growth and development of Helergen Solar Panels.

My CV is enclosed, and I would be happy to provide any further information you require.

I look forward to hearing from you.

Yours sincerely,

[signature here]

Malcolm Canmore

Some useful phrases

- I would like to be considered for the post of . . . , which your company advertised in . . .

- I would like to apply for the position of . . . as advertised in . . .

- I would like to be considered as an applicant for the post of . . .

- I am writing to apply for the position of . . .

- I am writing with regard to/in response to your company's advertisement for a . . . in the . . . , and I would like to apply for this position.

- I would like to apply for the above position.

- I would like to be considered for the above post.

- I would like to express my interest in . . .

- I was very pleased to see this vacancy advertised, as I . . .

- I have long wanted to work for . . . /work in the . . . sector.

- I believe that my experience as a . . . makes me a suitable candidate for this post.

- I believe I am a suitable candidate for this position because . . .

- I believe/am confident that I have the skills/experience/ qualifications required for this post.

- I believe that my skills/experience/qualifications would be of benefit to your organisation.

- I believe that my skills/experience/qualifications are a good match for the requirements/challenges of this post.

- I am confident that I could . . .

- I have a good knowledge/thorough understanding of . . .

- My experience as a . . . has given me the opportunity to become thoroughly familiar with . . .

- I have . . . years' experience in . . . / as a . . .

- I am an experienced . . .

- My qualifications/experience as a . . . would, I believe, make me an ideal person to fill this post.

- I am very much a team player.

- I am very much a self-starter and capable of working without supervision, but equally enjoy working as part of a team.

- I enjoy a challenge.

- I am used to working under pressure/to tight deadlines.

- I am a good communicator/experienced team leader.

- As you will see from my CV, which I have enclosed, . . .

- I enclose my CV for your consideration.

- My CV is enclosed.

- You will find my CV in an attachment to this email.

- Thank you for considering my application.

- I look forward to hearing from you.

- I look forward to meeting you in the near future.

- I would be pleased/available to attend an interview at your convenience.

- I would welcome the opportunity to discuss my suitability for the position with you.

- I look forward to discussing this employment opportunity with you.

- I would be glad to have the opportunity to discuss my application with you in more detail.

The CV

The second part of your job application is your CV. This gives a more detailed statement of your education, qualifications, experience, career, interests, etc. Like the covering letter, the CV has one main purpose: to make the person reading it sufficiently interested in you to offer you an interview. Your purpose in writing your CV, therefore, is to sell yourself. For this reason, you obviously want to highlight your strengths and play down (and avoid mentioning if possible) your weaknesses. You should also bear in mind that the person reading your letter and CV may have a large pile of applications to work through, so you need to make it as easy as possible for them to quickly find what you see as your key selling-points.

Opinions vary as to the correct form and layout of a good CV, but the one described below generally meets with approval. (Whole books have been devoted to the subject of writing CVs, and if you want further guidance *Perfect CV*, in the same series as this book, is recommended.) Whatever form your CV takes, some general points always apply:

- Your CV should be neat, clear and easy to read (more particularly, easy to scan quickly, as that is all the person reading it may have the time or inclination to do).

- The CV should be typed, on white A4 paper, on one side of the sheet only. Leave wide margins and plenty of white space on the sheet. (Obviously this does not apply exactly if you are submitting your CV by email, but the general principle holds good nevertheless.) It is better not to justify the lines (that is, make them all of the same length); lines of uneven length are more attractive.

- Unless you are absolutely sure that it is appropriate for the job you are applying for, do not try to draw attention to yourself or impress the reader by unconventional layouts, colours or typefaces. Keep to the conventional: a straightforward layout, with black ink on white paper, using a standard typeface in 11- or 12-point.

- Your CV should not be too long: two sheets of A4 (or its email equiv-alent) is good, three sheets is acceptable, four only if you really have a good reason for writing that much. Do not imagine that the more you write, the more impressed the reader is going to be; it doesn't work like that.

- Sentences and paragraphs should be fairly short. For most of your details, you don't need to write full sentences at all, just brief state-ments of fact (e.g. 'Clean driving licence' rather than 'I have a clean driving licence').

- As with your covering letter, your CV should be tailored to meet the requirements of each application you make. In any particular case, you may want to emphasise certain points while playing down others. (But do keep a note of which version of your CV you have sent to whom, so that if you do get invited to an interview, you know what the interviewer/panel has read.)

- Try to use words that have a positive connotation and emphasise (or at least imply) status and accomplishment. Among these are *achieved, attained, completed, controlled, designed, developed, exceeded, implemented, increased, ensured, led, managed, organised, planned, supervised.*

- Remember that your CV may form the basis of the discussion and questions you will face at your interview. Be prepared to talk about anything you mention, and don't mention anything you won't want to talk about.

- Lastly, but obviously, your CV should be carefully checked for spelling, grammar and punctuation errors.

The structure and content of your CV

1. Personal information
Begin the first page of your CV with your personal details: full name, address, email address if you have one, daytime telephone number.

- You may wish to include your nationality and your marital status, but these are not necessary and may not be helpful.

- Your date of birth is more problematic: if your age might count against you, you don't want to indicate it at the top of the first page. One way round this would be to limit the information you give at the top of the first page to your name, address, email address and phone number, and have a short section of 'Other personal information' slipped in somewhere at the bottom of the second or third page. By the time the reader has got that far, you will hopefully have so impressed them that your age won't matter!

- If you particularly want to draw attention to your qualifications, they also could be included in your personal details; it's probably not worth doing so for a single degree, though.

2. Personal profile

Your personal profile should follow your personal information. You use it to highlight your skills, experience, character, suitability, etc. This is the part of the CV where you sell yourself. Your personal profile should be no more than one or two paragraphs long.

3. Skills and achievements

In this section, you list any specific skills and achievements you have acquired during your career to date. Alternatively, you can simply include them as bullet points in your 'Employment' section. Or again, you might list your skills here and your achievements under Employment.

4. Résumé of employment

In the next section you list your current and/or previous employment.

- Begin with your current or most recent post, and work backwards.

- For each post, give a brief description or job title and outline your responsibilities and any related achievements you think worth mentioning.

- Since people read from left to right across the page, the best order of information is: what you did, for whom, and when. What you did is the key point you want to be noticed.

- Do not leave any unexplained gaps. If you took time out from your career for some reason, give details. (Again, if it is something you would prefer not to draw attention to, you might want to omit it in this section and explain it somewhere further on in your CV.)

- If you are starting out in your career, you could mention any part-time/temporary/voluntary jobs you had while at school, etc. If you are further on in your career, these are probably not relevant.

- Do not mention your current salary unless you are specifically asked for it.

5. Résumé of education

- As with your employment, begin with the most recent and work backwards.

- Again as with employment, since people read from left to right across the page, the best order of information is: what you got, where you got it, and when. The qualification gained is the key point you want to be noticed.

- It is not necessary or helpful to list every exam you have passed since you first set foot in school. If, for example, you have a degree, your school qualifications do not need to be listed in full. But do not omit any qualification or ability that might be a selling-point, such as knowledge of a foreign language.

6. Other information

Here you add any other *relevant* information about yourself. The information you provide here may, like what you have said about your career and education, form the basis of part of the interview. What you write here helps the interviewer to broaden the discussion beyond the limits of work and career, and to form a more rounded picture of you as a person.

- Among things to mention are membership of professional bodies, the holding of a clean driving licence (if that is relevant to the job), hobbies and interests, and voluntary work.

- Be selective. Only provide such information as is likely to further your cause, and try to avoid mentioning anything that won't.

- Think carefully before mentioning religious or political affiliations.

- Add 'References available on request'; there is no need to name your referees at this point.

A specimen CV

The following CV shows the general principles to be followed. Fit whatever you have to say about yourself into this broad structure:

Malcolm Canmore
7 Nonesuch Hill
Delmartin
Lincs DL3 9FR
Email: mcanmore29@anisp.co.uk
Tel: 01479 846200

Personal profile
I am a confident and experienced salesperson. A conscientious and highly motivated self-starter, I am flexible and work equally well on my own or as part of a team. I thrive under pressure, and I am used to meeting, and indeed exceeding, sales targets. I have excellent written and verbal communication skills, a relaxed personality, and a sense of humour, and have always developed a good rapport with my customers. I am keen to develop a career in the field of solar power, and consider that my several years' experience in plumbing and electrical wholesaling provides me with an ideal background for this.

Skills
Competent in the use of Uneke sales monitoring software.

Employment history

Senior sales executive	*Leadburn Plumbing &*	*2003 – present*
	Electrical Supplies	

- *Continued to develop my skills and experience as a sales executive.*
- *Trebled personal sales over the past four years.*
- *Twice winner of 'Sales Representative of the Year' award.*
- *Devised a new system of sales targeting and forecasting which has now been adopted by my current employers.*

Sales representative	*Watertite Roof Sealant Ltd, Leadburn*	*1996 – 2003*

- *Developed my skills and experience as a sales representative.*
- *Contributed to the threefold growth of the company.*

Education

Diploma in Marketing	*Leadburn Institute of Technology*	*1994 – 1996*
A level Mathematics, History + 6 GCSEs	*Sir William Barker's School, Leadburn*	*1987 – 1994*

Other information

- *Member of the Institute of Marketing.*
- *Clean driving licence; member of the Institute of Advanced Motorists.*
- *DoB: 4 May 1976.*
- *Married with two children.*
- *Interests include music and ancient history, and in addition I run a local youth theatre group.*
- *References available on request.*

Other employment-related letters

Accepting the offer of an interview

If the offer of an interview is made by email (as it may be), it is acceptable to reply by email.

Dear Mrs Seaton,

Area Sales Manager, SW England

Thank you for your letter of 17 November, inviting me for an interview in connection with the above position at your company office on Monday 6 December at 11 o'clock.

I confirm that I will be able to attend at that time, and look forward to meeting you then.

Yours sincerely, ...

Accepting the offer of a job

Dear Mrs Seaton,

Area Sales Manager, SW England

Thank you for your letter of 8 December, offering me the above position at an annual salary of £33,500.

I am very pleased to accept this position, and I understand that I am to begin on Monday 18 February 2011.

I am greatly looking forward to working for Helergen Solar Panels, and would like to thank you for giving me the opportunity of doing so.

Yours sincerely, ...

Declining the offer of a job

Dear Mrs Seaton,

Area Sales Manager, SW England

Thank you for your letter of 8 December, offering me the above position.

I would like to thank you for offering me the opportunity to work for Helergen Solar Panels, but after careful thought I have come to the conclusion that this would not be the correct career move for me at the present time and must therefore decline your offer.

It was a pleasure to meet you and other members of the Helergen board and staff. I wish you and the company every success in the future.

Yours sincerely, ...

Writing a reference

Normally a company will ask for references from a candidate's current employers or an educational institution that they have attended. However, it may be that you will find yourself in the position of being asked to provide a reference for someone you know. The letter you receive from the person's potential employer should make it clear what information is required, but the likelihood is that you will be being asked for a character reference, not an assessment of their knowledge, experience or ability.

The key points are: how long you have known the person, how well you know them, and how reliable, conscientious, etc you consider them to be. Keep your reply reasonably short and very much to the point, and don't get carried away.

Again we shall assume that it is Helergen Solar Panels that are seeking this information (but this time not about Malcolm Canmore):

Dear Mrs Seaton,

Frederick Moore, 26 Appleton Avenue

Thank you for your letter of 8 December, in which you ask for a character reference for Frederick.

I have known Fred for about fifteen years now. As you will realise from our respective addresses, I live two doors away from him and his mother, and ever since he was a small boy, he has been a frequent visitor to my house. I think I can therefore say that I know him well.

Fred has always been a polite and considerate boy. To give you just one example of this side to his character, when I was recently confined to my house due to illness, Fred visited me every day to inquire whether there was anything I needed, and I gather from his mother that it was he, not she, who suggested he did this. Although a quiet boy, he has always been popular with his peers and has many friends. He is conscientious and hard-working, and this shows in the excellent exam results he has achieved this year and that I am sure you are already aware of.

I hope this is of help to you. Please do not hesitate to contact me again if you require any further information.

Yours sincerely, ...

(A reference of this sort might also be required for someone who is wanting to rent accommodation.)

Letter of resignation

The final employment-related letter we have to deal with is the resignation letter. At its most basic, all you have to say in your letter is that you are leaving, and when, but you will probably want to say more than that.

- You do not have to give any reason for your resignation, but you may wish to do so, or you may prefer to leave this to a face-to-face conversation with your personnel manager (or whoever).

- If you have been happy in the company, you should probably say so. You may, for example, wish to thank them for the support they have given you during your time with them, and the opportunities you have had to develop your career.

- If you are leaving because you are unhappy in your present job, there is no reason not to say so, but be very careful not to say anything offensive or libellous: as you move around in your career, so may others you are currently working with, and chickens can come home to roost. If you have criticisms to make, be factual and measured in your comments, and don't let anger, bitterness or perhaps career disappointment lead you to say something you will regret later. If you have never got on well with your line manager, what does it matter now? Let it be.

- Wish the company success for the future (even if you are going to work for a competitor!).

- Your letter need not be unnaturally formal (though there may be some formal official phrases in it). Depending on the size of the company and your relationship with the person you are writing to, you can address them by their first name or by their title and surname.

Dear Ken,

As you know from our conversation yesterday, I have accepted the post of SW England Area Sales Manager with Helergen Solar Panels. I am therefore writing to you to officially tender my resignation from Leadburn Plumbing & Electrical Supplies. In accordance with the terms of my contract, I am giving you four weeks' notice and will be leaving the company on Friday 1 February.

I have very much enjoyed my seven years with LPES, and have appreciated the support and friendship of all my colleagues here. I cannot pretend that I won't miss you all, but it seemed to be the right time for me to move on in my career, and as you know I have for a long time now had an interest in the development of renewable energy.

Over the next few weeks, I will do all I can to facilitate the handover to those who will for the time being be taking on my roles and responsibilities.

I wish LPES every success for the future.

Yours sincerely,

Malcolm

Some useful phrases

- I wish to resign from my post as . . .

- I am writing to resign (from) my position with the company/my position as . . .

- I hereby tender my resignation as of . . .

- Please accept this letter as my formal notice of resignation.

- I would like to ask the company to waive the four weeks' notice required by my contract.

- Although I am aware that my contract stipulates four weeks' notice of leaving, I would like to ask the company to allow me to leave at an earlier date.

- Would the company be willing to waive this notice period/allow me to leave at an earlier date?

14 Seeking sponsorship or donations

Asking for money is never easy, but it is sometimes necessary. Perhaps you work for a charity or belong to a community group or faith group, and you have a project for which funds are needed. Or perhaps you are planning as an individual to undertake some activity (a bike ride, a marathon, etc) in aid of charity. Or again it may be that it is not money but some other sort of contribution you are looking for. In any case, there are people out there who would be willing to help, but they won't unless they are asked, and you have to ask them. Your appeal letter needs to be both well thought out and well set out; it must be easy to read, not too long, and clear in its objectives.

Whoever you approach and for whatever reason, six possible key points for your letter are:

- what you want (money or something else),

- why you want it (what your appeal is for and why it is necessary),

- when you want it,

- the total amount of money you are hoping to raise,

- what the money will be spent on,

- who will benefit from it.

In addition, if you are appealing on behalf of an organisation, you should state clearly what it is and what your role in it is. If your organisation is not likely to be known to your target sponsor or contributor, you should give some background information about what it does and who its activities support. If your organisation has a charity number, make sure you include it in the heading or at the foot of the appeal letter.

As an effective means of indicating the value of your organisation's work or gaining sympathy for it, you might illustrate your appeal letter with appropriate photographs or drawings. You could also add a quote or two from some of those who will benefit from whatever the money raised is to be spent on; bringing your project or activity to life in this way is an important selling-point. And you should consider targeting people or organisations who you know or expect to have some connection with, interest in or sympathy for your organisation or intended charity and the work it does. If possible, address your letter to a named individual.

The following are two examples of the sort of letter you might send out:

Mr G Martin
The Blue Boar Inn
12 The Green
Lower Oakton

Dear Mr Martin,

The local playgroup is in great need of new outdoor equipment for the thirty or so children we cater for in our Mothers and Toddlers Group and our Primary After-School Group. As the two groups have grown over the years, we find that the equipment we have is no longer sufficient for our needs, and moreover much of it is now well past its best and really ought to be replaced. We estimate that we will require something in the region of £3,000 to purchase suitable new equipment.

For this reason the playgroup parents committee is organising a number of fund-raising events in the coming months, one of which will be a raffle which we hope to hold next month. We are therefore approaching local traders such as yourself to ask whether you would be willing to contribute a prize for this raffle. In your case, we were hoping that you might agree to offer dinner for two at the Blue Boar.

So far the response has been very good, and we hope you too will be willing to support us in this venture, which is so important for the children of the village.

I look forward to hearing from you.

Yours sincerely,

[signature here]

Marjory Ure (Mrs),
Secretary,
White Mice Playgroup Parents Committee

Mrs M Gibson
Graham & Martin plc
23 Bridge Street
Newton Brackby

Dear Mrs Gibson,

My name is Timothy Fenton, and I am a member of the 31st Newton Brackby Scout Group. I have recently been accepted as a participant in a two-week international scout jamboree that will be held in Canada in July next year. I will in fact be the only scout from this county who will be participating in the jamboree.

Potential participants in jamborees such as this have to participate in an assessment weekend before being accepted, and given the competition that there was for places, I feel honoured to have been selected as one of the British representatives. Participation in this jamboree will afford me a unique opportunity to forge friendships with scouts from many other countries, and I am very much looking forward to widening in this way my knowledge and understanding of life in many parts of the world that I could never expect to visit for myself.

Naturally, travel to and participation in an event such as this is expensive, and British participants will have to pay something in the region of £1,100. (We will not know the exact figure until nearer the time.) I am therefore currently looking for financial sponsors to help me with the costs of this venture.

Would it be possible for Graham & Martin to assist me by making a contribution to these costs? Any sum your firm was willing to contribute would be very much appreciated.

Please feel free to contact me if you need any further information.

Yours sincerely,

[signature here]

Timothy Fenton

Quick Reference 1
Abbreviations frequently used in addresses

Abbreviations in addresses

Streets and buildings

These are generally written without final full stops nowadays.

Apt	Apartment
Ave, Av	Avenue
Bldg	Building
Blvd	Boulevard
Cl	Close
Cres	Crescent
Ct	Court
Dr	Drive
Est	Estate
Gdns	Gardens
Gr	Grove
Hse	House
La	Lane
Mt	Mount
Pde	Parade

Pk	Park
Pl	Place
Plz	Plaza
Rd	Road
Rm	Room
Sq	Square
St	Street
Terr	Terrace
Vw	View

In some towns and cities, the address of a flat may be given as, for example, '2F1', which means 'flat 1 on the 2nd floor'.

English counties

'Co.' or 'Co' is the abbreviation for 'County' in addresses: *Co. Durham*. Abbreviated county names are usually written without final full stops.

Bedfordshire	Beds
Berkshire	Berks
Buckinghamshire	Bucks
Cambridgeshire	Cambs
Derbyshire	Derbys, Derbs
Gloucestershire	Glos, Gloucs
Hampshire	Hants
Hertfordshire	Herts
Lancashire	Lancs
Leicestershire	Leics

Lincolnshire	Lincs
Middlesex	Middx
Northamptonshire	Northants
Nottinghamshire	Notts
Oxfordshire	Oxon
Shropshire	Shrops, Salop
Wiltshire	Wilts
Worcestershire	Worcs
Yorkshire	Yorks

American states

Alabama	AL
Alaska	AK
Arizona	AZ
Arkansas	AR
California	CA
Colorado	CO
Connecticut	CT
Delaware	DE
District of Columbia	DC
Florida	FL
Georgia	GA
Hawaii	HI
Idaho	ID
Illinois	IL
Indiana	IN
Iowa	IA

Kansas	KS
Kentucky	KY
Louisiana	LA
Maine	ME
Maryland	MD
Massachusetts	MA
Michigan	MI
Minnesota	MN
Mississippi	MS
Missouri	MO
Montana	MT
Nebraska	NE
Nevada	NV
New Hampshire	NH
New Jersey	NJ
New Mexico	NM
New York	NY
North Carolina	NC
North Dakota	ND
Ohio	OH
Oklahoma	OK
Oregon	OR
Pennsylvania	PA
Rhode Island	RI
South Carolina	SC
South Dakota	SD
Tennessee	TN
Texas	TX

Utah	UT
Vermont	VT
Virginia	VA
Washington	WA
West Virginia	WV
Wisconsin	WI
Wyoming	WY

Canadian provinces and territories

Alberta	AB
British Columbia	BC
Manitoba	MB
New Brunswick	NB
Newfoundland and Labrador	NL
Northwest Territories	NT
Nova Scotia	NS
Nunavut	NU
Ontario	ON
Prince Edward Island	PE
Quebec	QC
Saskatchewan	SK
Yukon	YT

Australian states and territories

Australian Capital Territory	ACT
New South Wales	NSW
Northern Territory	NT
Queensland	QLD
South Australia	SA
Tasmania	TAS
Victoria	VIC
Western Australia	WA

Quick Reference 2
Correct forms of address for letters and envelopes

The following entries show you how to address, open and close a letter to someone who holds an official rank or title.

The following points should be noted:

- In the forms of address given in this section, F– stands for 'forename' and S– for 'surname'.

- Where a few titles are given followed by 'etc', e.g. 'Mr/Mrs/Sir (etc)', the correct title of the person you are writing to should of course be used.

- In some cases, there are more formal versions of salutation and complimentary close, but these are no longer considered necessary. While some of the forms suggested here may seem to you more formal or florid than you would choose to use, it is generally best to keep to convention with formal letters. For further information, see for example *Debrett's Correct Form* in your local library, or search online for 'correct forms of address'.

- Some of the forms of address given below for letters and envelopes should be split over two lines: e.g. 'The Rt Hon. F– S–, MP, Secretary of State for Communities and Local Government' would be written as

    'The Rt Hon. F– S–, MP
    Secretary of State for Communities and Local Government'

Use your judgement over this, making sure lines are well-balanced.

Ambassador, British

Address on letter/envelope: HE Mr/Mrs/Sir (etc) F– S–
(HE = 'His/Her Excellency')
Begin letter with: Dear Ambassador
Close letter with: Believe me, my dear Ambassador, Yours sincerely, . . .;
less formally Yours sincerely, . . .

Ambassador, Foreign

Address on letter/envelope: HE Mr/Mrs (etc) F– S–, the . . . Ambassador
or the Ambassador of . . .; *alternatively* HE the . . . Ambassador *or* HE
the Ambassador of . . .
Begin letter with: Dear Ambassador
Close letter with: Believe me, my dear Ambassador, Yours sincerely; *less
formally* Yours sincerely

Archbishop (Anglican)

Address on letter/envelope: The Most Rev. the Lord Archbishop of . . .
(The Archbishops of Canterbury and York should be addressed as 'The
Most Rev. and Rt Hon. the Lord Archbishop of . . .'.)
Begin letter with: Dear Archbishop; *more formally* Dear Lord
Archbishop
Close letter with: Yours sincerely

Archbishop (Roman Catholic)

Address on letter/envelope: His Grace the Archbishop of . . .
Begin letter with: Dear Archbishop; *more formally* Dear Lord
Archbishop
Close letter with: Yours sincerely

Archdeacon

Address on letter/envelope: The Ven. the Archdeacon of . . .
(Ven. = 'Venerable')
Begin letter with: Dear Archdeacon
Close letter with: Yours sincerely

Baron

Address on letter/envelope: The Lord S–
Begin letter with: Dear Lord S–
Close letter with: Yours sincerely

Baroness (wife of baron)

Address on letter/envelope: The Lady S–
Begin letter with: Dear Lady S–
Close letter with: Yours sincerely

Baroness (in her own right)

Address on letter/envelope: The Lady S– *or* The Baroness S–
Begin letter with: Dear Lady S– *or* Dear Baroness S–
Close letter with: Yours sincerely

Baronet

Address on letter/envelope: Sir F– S–, Bt
Begin letter with: Dear Sir F–
Close letter with: Yours sincerely

Baronet's wife

Address on letter/envelope: Lady S–
Begin letter with: Dear Lady S–
Close letter with: Yours sincerely

Bishop (Anglican)

Address on letter/envelope: The Rt Rev. the Lord Bishop of . . .
(The Bishop of London should be addressed as 'The Rt Rev. and Rt Hon.
the Lord Bishop of London'.)
Begin letter with: Dear Bishop *or* Dear Lord Bishop
Close letter with: Yours sincerely

Bishop (Roman Catholic)

Address on letter/envelope: The Rt Rev. F– S–, Bishop of . . .
(Irish bishops are 'Most Rev.' rather than 'Rt Rev.', and are given the
courtesy title of 'Dr'.)

Begin letter with: Dear Bishop
Close letter with: Yours sincerely

Cabinet Minister *see* Secretary of State

Canon (Anglican)
Address on letter/envelope: The Rev. Canon F– S–
Begin letter with: Dear Canon S–
Close letter with: Yours sincerely

Cardinal
Address on letter/envelope: His Eminence Cardinal F– S– *or* His
Eminence the Cardinal Archbishop of . . .
Begin letter with: Dear Cardinal; *more formally* Your Eminence
Close letter with: Yours sincerely

Chief Rabbi
Address on letter/envelope: The Very Rev. the Chief Rabbi *or* The Chief
Rabbi Mr/Sir F– S–
Begin letter with: Dear Chief Rabbi
Close letter with: Yours sincerely

Clergy (Anglican and Protestant Churches)
Address on letter/envelope: The Rev. F– S–
Begin letter with: Dear Mr/Mrs (etc) S–
(While it is correct to address a member of the clergy as 'Rev. S–' in
American English, it is not correct to do so in British English.)
Close letter with: Yours sincerely

Clergy (Roman Catholic)
Address on letter/envelope: The Rev. F– S– *or* The Rev. Fr S–
(If he is a member of a religious order, the initials of the order should be
added after the name; e.g. 'The Rev. F– S–, OSB'.)
Begin letter with: Dear Father S–
Close letter with: Yours sincerely

Councillor

Address on letter/envelope: (if a man) Councillor F– S–; (if a woman) Councillor Mrs/Miss (etc) F– S–

Begin letter with: Dear Councillor S– *or* Dear Mr/Mrs (etc) S–

Close letter with: Yours sincerely

Countess

Address on letter/envelope: The Rt Hon. the Countess of . . .; *less formally* The Countess of . . .

Begin letter with: Dear Lady . . .

Close letter with: Yours sincerely

Dame

Address on letter/envelope: Dame F– S–

(The name should be followed by the initials of the Order of Chivalry to which the dame belongs; e.g. 'Dame F– S–, DCVO'.)

Begin letter with: Dear Dame F–

Close letter with: Yours sincerely

Dean (Anglican)

Address on letter/envelope: The Very Rev. the Dean of . . .

Begin letter with: Dear Dean

Close letter with: Yours sincerely

Duchess

Address on letter/envelope: Her Grace the Duchess of . . .; *less formally* The Duchess of . . .

Begin letter with: Dear Duchess

Close letter with: Yours sincerely

Duke

Address on letter/envelope: His Grace the Duke of . . .; *less formally* The Duke of . . .

Begin letter with: Dear Duke

Close letter with: Yours sincerely

Earl

Address on letter/envelope: The Rt Hon. the Earl of . . .; *less formally* The Earl of . . .
Begin letter with: Dear Lord . . .
Close letter with: Yours sincerely

First Minister (Scotland/Wales/Northern Ireland)

Address on letter/envelope: The Rt Hon. F– S–, MSP/AM/MLA, First Minister
Begin letter with: Dear First Minister *or* Dear Mr/Mrs (etc) S–
Close letter with: Yours sincerely

Governor (US State)

Address on letter/envelope: The Hon. F– S–, Governor of . . .
Begin letter with: Dear Governor S–
Close letter with: Yours sincerely

Imam

Address on letter/envelope: Mr/Dr F– S–; *or simply* The Imam, . . . Mosque
Begin letter with: Dear Mr/Dr S– *or* Dear Imam
Close letter with: Yours sincerely

Judge (High Court)

Address on letter/envelope: The Hon. Mr/Mrs Justice S–
(Write 'Mrs' even if the lady in question is unmarried.)
Begin letter with: My Lord/Lady (if writing about judicial matters); *less formally* Dear Sir F–/Dame F– *or even* Dear Judge
Close letter with: Yours faithfully (if opening with 'My Lord/Lady'); *otherwise* Yours sincerely

Judge, Circuit

Address on letter/envelope: His/Her Honour Judge S–
(If the judge has been a QC, add 'QC' after the name.)
Begin letter with: Dear Sir/Madam; *less formally* Dear Judge

Close letter with: Yours faithfully (if opening with 'Dear Sir/Madam'); *otherwise* Yours sincerely

Knight

Address on letter/envelope: Sir F– S–

(The name should be followed by the initials of the Order of Chivalry to which the knight belongs, e.g. 'Sir F– S–, KCMG'; some knights, 'Knights Bachelor', have no letters after their name. If an envelope is addressed to a knight and his wife, it should read 'Sir F– and Lady S–'.)

Begin letter with: Dear Sir F–

Close letter with: Yours sincerely

Lady (wife of knight)

Address on letter/envelope: Lady S–

(The wife of a knight is not addressed as 'Lady F– S–' unless she is the daughter of a duke, a marquess or an earl.)

Begin letter with: Dear Lady S–

Close letter with: Yours sincerely

Life Peer/Peeress

Address on letter/envelope: The Lord/Lady S–

Begin letter with: Dear Lord/Lady S–

Close letter with: Yours sincerely

Minister (Government)

Address on letter/envelope: F– S–, MP, Minister of State, Department of . . .

Begin letter with: Dear Mr/Mrs (etc) S– *or* Dear Minister

Close letter with: Yours sincerely

Minister (Religious) *see* Clergy

Lord Mayor/Provost

Address on letter/envelope: The Lord Mayor/Lord Provost of . . .

(The Lord Mayors of London, York, Belfast, Cardiff and Dublin, and the

Lord Provosts of Edinburgh and Glasgow, are addressed as 'The Rt Hon. the Lord Mayor/Lord Provost of . . .'.)
Begin letter with: Dear Lord Mayor/Provost
(Use 'Lord' even if the holder of the office is a woman; a 'Lady Mayoress' or 'Lady Provost' is the wife of a Lord Mayor/Provost.)
Close letter with: Yours sincerely

Marchioness

Address on letter/envelope: The Most Hon. the Marchioness of . . .; *less formally* The Marchioness of . . .
Begin letter with: Dear Lady . . .
Close letter with: Yours sincerely

Marquess

Address on letter/envelope: The Most Hon. the Marquess of . . .; *less formally* The Marquess of . . .
(Some Scottish marquesses use the spelling 'marquis'.)
Begin letter with: Dear Lord . . .
Close letter with: Yours sincerely

Mayor

Address on letter/envelope: The Mayor of . . .
Begin letter with: Dear Mr/Madam Mayor *or* Dear Mr/Mrs (etc) S–
(It is correct to use 'Mr Mayor' even if the holder of the office is a woman, though female mayors often prefer 'Madam Mayor' and in the 21st century this really has to be considered the preferable form for addressing a woman. A 'mayoress' is usually the wife of a mayor, not a female mayor.)
Close letter with: Yours sincerely

Member of Parliament/Assembly

Address on letter/envelope: Mr/Mrs/Dr (etc) S–, MP/MEP/MSP/AM/MLA (as appropriate)
Begin letter with: Dear Mr/Mrs/Dr (etc) S–
Close letter with: Yours sincerely

Monsignor

Address on letter/envelope: The Rev. Monsignor F– S–
Begin letter with: Dear Monsignor S–
Close letter with: Yours sincerely

Officers in the Armed Forces

Address on letter/envelope: Major/Admiral/Squadron Leader (etc) F– S–
(The professional rank precedes any other rank or title: e.g. 'Colonel the
Rt Hon. Sir F– S–' or 'Colonel the Rt Hon. the Viscount S–'. Retired
officers above the rank of Lieutenant in the Royal Navy, above the rank
of Captain in the Army and above the rank of Flight Lieutenant in
the Royal Air Force may continue to use and be addressed by the rank
they held while in service; also cavalry officers of the rank of Captain if
they continue to work with horses.)
Begin letter with: Dear Major/Admiral/Squadron Leader (etc) S–
Close letter with: Yours sincerely

Pope

Address on letter/envelope: His Holiness the Pope
Begin letter with: Your Holiness *or* Most Holy Father
Close letter with: (for Roman Catholics) I have the honour to be Your
Holiness's most devoted and obedient child; (for others) I have the
honour to be Your Holiness's obedient servant
(If you are not a Roman Catholic, you might consider the above formu-
lae inappropriate, but it is probably best to keep to convention; 'Dear
Pope F–' and 'Yours sincerely' could be considered too informal, unless
you really feel uncomfortable with the standard phrases.)

President of the United States of America

Address on letter/envelope: The President *or* The Hon. F– S–, President
of the United States
(Send to 'The White House'.)
Begin letter with: Dear Mr/Madam President
Close letter with: Yours sincerely

Prime Minister

Address on letter/envelope: The Rt Hon. F– S–, MP, Prime Minister
Begin letter with: Dear Prime Minister *or* Dear Mr/Mrs (etc) S–
Close letter with: Yours sincerely

Prince/Princess

Address on letter/envelope: the letter should not be addressed directly to the Prince or Princess but to their private secretary; for example, 'The Private Secretary to His Royal Highness The Prince of Wales', 'The Private Secretary to Her Royal Highness The Duchess of Cornwall, 'The Private Secretary to Her Royal Highness The Princess Royal, KG, KT, GCVO', etc (Check reliable sources, such as *Debrett*, for the correct form for whichever member of the Royal Family you are writing to.)
Begin letter with: Dear Sir
Close letter with: Yours faithfully

Provost *see* Mayor

Queen

Address on letter/envelope: a letter to the Queen should be addressed to 'The Private Secretary to Her Majesty The Queen', not directly to the Queen
Begin letter with: Dear Sir
Close letter with: Yours faithfully

Rabbi

Address on letter/envelope: The Rev. Rabbi F– S–
Begin letter with: Dear Rabbi S–
(If the rabbi is a doctor, address as 'The Rev. Rabbi Dr F– S–' and begin 'Dear Dr S–'.)
Close letter with: Yours sincerely

Representative (US House of Congress)

Address on letter/envelope: The Hon. F– S–, Member, United States House of Representatives

Begin letter with: Dear Representative S– *or* Dear Congressman/Congresswoman S–

Close letter with: Yours sincerely

Secretary of State (United Kingdom)

Address on letter/envelope: The Rt Hon. F– S–, MP, Secretary of State for . . .

Begin letter with: Dear Chancellor, Dear Home/Foreign/Justice (etc) Secretary *or* (if the title would be too cumbersome) Dear Secretary of State; *alternatively* Dear Mr/Mrs (etc) S–

Close letter with: Yours sincerely

Senator (US Federal)

Address on letter/envelope: The Hon. F– S–, United States Senator

Begin letter with: Dear Senator S–

Close letter with: Yours sincerely

Viscount

Address on letter/envelope: The Rt Hon. the Viscount . . .; *less formally* Viscount . . .

Begin letter with: Dear Lord . . .

Close letter with: Yours sincerely

Viscountess

Address on letter/envelope: The Rt Hon. the Viscountess . . .; *less formally* Viscountess . . .

Begin letter with: Dear Lady . . .

Close letter with: Yours sincerely

Watch your language!

No matter how well written your letter looks, if it has errors of language in it then it certainly isn't perfect. Your letters must be grammatically correct and well punctuated, and they must use the correct words correctly spelt. This section will help you through the language minefield.

Of course, there is only enough room here to cover the basic rules and the commonest and most serious errors. If you need more information, you should look for a book on 'good English' or 'better English' that covers correct English usage in more detail. (Two books that you might find useful are *Perfect Punctuation* and *Perfect Written English*.) You should also have a good dictionary, to check the meanings and spelling of words you are not sure about.

Punctuation

Full stop

- A full stop is used at the end of a sentence (except for questions and exclamations).

- A full stop is used after an abbreviation, nowadays in British English usually only after an abbreviation that does not include the last letter of the abbreviated word: *Co.*, *etc.*, *i.e.*, *Sq.* but *Dr*, *Mr*, *Mrs*, *Rd*

- Abbreviations consisting of capital letters are written without full stops: *AGM, BBC, CV, MP, NATO, USA, W* (for 'west')

- Abbreviations of degrees and honours are usually written without full stops: *BSc, MA, OBE, VC*

Question mark

- A question mark is used at the end of a sentence that asks a question: *Where is she going?* ◆ *I wonder if you could tell me the way to the station?*

- A question mark should not be used with a sentence that does not actually ask a question: *Ask her where she is going.* ◆ *Could you please pass me the marmalade.*

Exclamation mark

- An exclamation mark is used to express strong emphasis or emotion: *It wasn't me!* ◆ *What a mess!*

- It is best not to use more than one exclamation mark in anything other than very informal writing: *It wasn't me!!!*

- Note that some sentences that look like questions are in fact exclamations: *What are you doing!* ◆ *Will you stop doing that!*

Comma

- A comma marks a slight break or pause in a sentence: *Damaged by the wind, the roof collapsed.* ◆ *Seeing him there, she turned and fled.* ◆ *As everybody knows, the world is getting warmer.* ◆ *Run for it, James!* ◆ *That's a bit of a mess, isn't it?* ◆ *Yes, we can come on Sunday.* ◆ *Thank you, we'd love to come.* ◆ *I don't need any help, thank you.*

- Notice the difference in punctuation between *I'll phone you as soon as I arrive* (with no pause in the sentence and therefore no comma) and *As soon as I arrive, I'll phone you* (with a comma to mark the slight pause). The same rule applies in *I have no idea what he was doing in the garden* and *What he was doing in the garden, I have no idea.*

- When a word or phrase is inserted into the middle of a sentence, you need two commas round it: *The world, as everybody knows, is getting warmer.* ◆ *You, Mary, should stay here.* ◆ *We, on the other hand, can leave immediately.* ◆ *That, however, is a different matter.*

- Information that points to a particular person or thing is not separated off by commas: *The boy who had kicked the cat ran away* (i.e. that particular boy). Information that is simply given as an extra comment is separated off by commas: *The boy, who had kicked the cat, ran away.* ◆ *John, Susan's brother, is a policeman.*

- A comma replaces a full stop in reported speech if the 'saying' word follows what is said: *'I will come back tomorrow,' said Tom.* Note the different punctuation when the 'saying' word comes before what is said: *Tom said, 'I will come back tomorrow.'*

- You need two commas if the 'saying' word comes in the middle of a sentence: *'I will,' Tom said, 'come back tomorrow.'*

- A question mark or exclamation mark is not replaced by a comma: *'Who was that?' asked John.*

- When a series of similar words or phrases occur together as a sort of list, they are separated by commas: *Eagles, buzzards, hawks and falcons are all birds of prey.* ◆ *The garden was full of red, orange, yellow and pink flowers.* ◆ *Some of the people in the crowd were laughing, some were cheering, some were crying, some were waving flags.*

- A comma may optionally be inserted before the 'and': *Eagles, buzzards, hawks, and falcons are all birds of prey.*

- When two words together form a single item, do not insert a comma: *a pretty little girl* (= a little girl who is pretty)

Semicolon

- A semicolon is used to separate word-groups that could be treated as separate sentences (ending in full stops) but which you want to link more closely into a single sentence: *The war ended; people returned to their homes; life began again.*

- Semicolons are used instead of commas in sentences where a succession of commas might be confusing or to clearly group some parts of the sentence into separate units: *The company has offices in Lima, Peru; Caracas, Venezuela; and Belem, in Brazil.* ♦ *In the garden was a flower-bed with roses, delphiniums and potentilla; a vegetable garden with peas, beans and radishes; and a privet hedge intertwined with honeysuckle.*

- A semicolon may introduce something that expands on or contrasts with what has gone before: *No one said a word; we were all waiting to see what would happen.* ♦ *My wife likes avocados; I can't stand them.*

Colon

- A colon may introduce part of a sentence that expands on or explains what has preceded it: *One thing is for sure: we are not leaving.*

- A colon may introduce a list: *You need the following equipment: a saw, a hammer, chisels and sandpaper.*

- A colon may introduce a quotation or quoted speech: *As Donne once said: 'No man is an island.'*

- A colon may indicate a strong contrast: *Man hopes: God knows.*

Dash

- Dashes are used to separate off additional comments in a sentence: *Looking back – hindsight is a wonderful thing! – I realise I should have left right away.*

- Just as a colon may introduce a list, a dash may follow a list: *A saw, a hammer, chisels and sandpaper – these are all the tools you will need.*

- A dash is used when there is an abrupt break in a sentence: *If only I had told Mary what I – oh, but what's the use of thinking about that now?*

- A dash is used to link words or numbers to show a range or extent: *the 1914–1918 war* ✦ *the Paris–Dakar race* ✦ *pages 1–23*

- Do not combine dashes with words such as 'from' or 'between'. Do not, for example, write *from 1914–1918* or *between 1914–1918*; write *from 1914 to 1918* and *between 1914 and 1918*.

Parentheses

- Like dashes, parentheses are used to separate off additional comments in a sentence: *Looking back (hindsight is a wonderful thing!), I realise I should have left right away.*

Inverted commas or quotation marks

- Quotation marks are placed around direct speech: *'Where are we?' asked Sue.*

- Sentence punctuation marks go *inside* speech quotation marks: *'I am not,' said Mr Jones, 'very happy about this.'* ✦ *'Don't leave me!' she screamed. 'Why are you doing this?'*

- Quotation marks are also used to pick out or highlight words in a sentence, such as titles or quoted words: *He's appearing in 'Hamlet' at the Old Theatre.*

- Sentence punctuation marks go *outside* highlighting quotation marks: *This is really not 'the done thing'.*

- Single quotation marks ('. . .') are now generally preferred to double quotation marks (". . .") in British English.

- If you need quotation marks in a sentence that is already in quotation marks, then use double quotes within single ones: *'What does "binary" mean?' asked Tim.*

Apostrophe

- The apostrophe is used to mark possessive forms of nouns: *John's books* ◆ *James's books* ◆ *the boy's books* (= the books belonging to the boy) ◆ *the children's books* (= the books belonging to the children) ◆ *the boys' books* (= the books belonging to the boys)

- With names ending in *-s*, usage varies: both *Moses' army* and *Moses's army* are correct.

- An apostrophe should not normally be used to indicate a plural noun: write *apples and bananas*, not *apple's and banana's*.

- The plurals of some short words are, or can be, written with apostrophes: *do's* (or *dos*) *and don'ts.* ◆ *There are really two me's: the quiet me and the crazy me.*

- The plurals of words that are picked out or quoted in a sentence may be written with apostrophes: *There are too many if's and but's in this contract.*

- Apostrophes are used to show where letters have been omitted: *we'll* (= we will) ◆ *can't* (= cannot).

Hyphen

- A hyphen should be used in a descriptive phrase that precedes the noun it describes: *a long-term solution* ◆ *a no-risk offer* ◆ *a four-wheel-drive, off-road vehicle* ◆ *one of our best-loved actors* ◆ *She had a don't-dare-argue-with-me look on her face.*

- Hyphens are used in many compound nouns: *brother-in-law* ◆ *half-truth.* There is no easy rule for this: check in a dictionary if you are not sure whether or not to use a hyphen.

- Do not use a hyphen in a phrasal verb, such as *get away, pay in, sell out.* You should, however, hyphenate nouns derived from phrasal verbs: *a pay-in* ◆ *a sell-out.* Some nouns are written as single words without hyphens: *a getaway.* Here again, check in a dictionary.

Some essential points of grammar

... and I or ... and me?

Constructions such as *between you and I, for you and I, with you and I* are grammatically incorrect. The correct phrases are *between you and me, for you and me, with you and me* (just as you would say *for me, with me*, etc).

Similarly, you should use *and me* rather than *and I* after a verb: *The old lady gave Tim and me 50p each* (just as you would say *The old lady gave me 50p*). But before a verb you should say *and I*: *My brother and I both support Arsenal* (just as you would say *I support Arsenal*).

... as good or better than ...

Many people do not notice that there is a word missing in a construction such as this. It is not correct to say that one thing is *as good or better than* something else; you must say that it is *as good as or better than* the other: *Some British wines are as good as or better than French wines.* Similarly: *The situation is as bad as, or worse than, it was six months ago.*

Double negative

In standard English, constructions with two negative words such as *I didn't do nothing* are ungrammatical. The correct form is *I didn't do anything, I can't see anyone*, etc.

fewer or less?

Use *fewer* with plural nouns: *fewer cars, fewer mistakes*. Use *less* with singular nouns: *less hassle, less waste*.

he or she or they?

Some people object to the use of *they* as a singular pronoun meaning 'he or she': *A teacher must always do what they think best for their students no matter what the government tells them to do.* It is probably wise, therefore, to avoid this usage if you can in important letters and documents. What are the alternatives?

- The best way is to make the whole sentence plural: *Teachers must always do what they think best for their students no matter what the government tells them to do.*

- You can use *he or she,* but this can become cumbersome if you then have to use *him or her* and *his or hers* in the same sentence: *A teacher must always do what he or she thinks best for his or her students no matter what the government tells him or her to do.*

- It is best not to use abbreviated forms such as *s/he.*

It was me/him

Expressions such as *It's me, It was her,* etc are grammatically correct. But when the pronouns *I/me, he/him, she/her,* etc are linked to a following clause, the grammar is a little more complicated; it depends on who did what to whom:

- Corresponding to a sentence *He scared the cat,* it is perfectly acceptable to say either *It was him who scared the cat* or, in more formal English, *It was he who scared the cat.* Similarly, you can say *It was me who phoned* or, more formally, *It was I who phoned.*

- Corresponding to a sentence *The cat scared him,* you should say *It was him the cat scared.* Similarly, you should say *It was probably her you saw* corresponding to *You probably saw her.*

may have and might have

May have is now often used where *might have* would be more correct. *May have* implies that something is possible but you are not sure about it: *The dog may have run in front of the car* (i.e. it is possible that the dog ran in front of the car, but you do not know whether it did or not). *Might have* can also have this meaning: *I suppose the dog might have run in front of the car.* However, *might have,* but not *may have,* can also refer to something that could have happened but that you know did not happen: *If the dog had not been on a lead, it might have run in front of the car.*

me writing or my writing?

Should you say *I hope you don't mind me writing to you* or *I hope you don't mind my writing to you*? In fact, both are acceptable, though some people think that the first construction (with *me*) is incorrect. The second construction (with *my*) may be preferred in formal English, but otherwise it is an issue that is really not worth worrying about.

Misrelated participle

Strictly speaking, a participle in a subordinate clause relates to the subject of the main clause: *Sheltering under a tree, Tim watched a flock of ducks fly past* (i.e., it was Tim who was sheltering under the tree). Sentences in which the participle does not relate to the subject of the main clause are ungrammatical, and sometimes rather comical: *Sheltering under a tree, Tim's hat blew away.* (It wasn't Tim's hat that was sheltering under the tree.) ◆ *While driving through the field, a cow ran into him.* (It wasn't the cow that was driving through the field.) Although it is probable that most people will not notice this mistake, it does really irritate some people and it is therefore best to avoid it in important documents such as job applications and CVs. A correct version of the last example would be *While he was driving through the field, a cow ran into him.*

none

Contrary to what some people think, it is not wrong to follow *none* with a plural verb: *None of the parcels have arrived.* A singular verb is also possible in many cases (e.g. *None of the cars is equipped with satnav*), but a plural verb is much more common.

Split infinitive

A 'split infinitive' is a phrase in which a word comes between *to* and a following verb: *to boldly go*, *to clearly see*. These constructions are perfectly grammatical, but unfortunately many people have been taught in school that they are not grammatically correct, so it is wise to avoid them in important documents such as job applications and CVs.

... than I/he or ... than me/him?

When a verb follows the pronoun in constructions with *than*, you have to use the *I/he/she* form of the pronoun with no following verb: *My wife eats more than I do, but I drink more than she does.* Where there is no following verb, it is normal in everyday English to use the *me/him/her* form of the pronoun: *My wife eats more than me, but I drink more than her.* Only in very formal English would you use the *I/he/she* form of the pronoun with no following verb: *My wife eats more than I, but I drink more than she.* However, you must watch out for ambiguities. If you say *My wife likes Josh Groban more than me*, it is not clear whether you mean she likes Josh Groban more than you like Josh Groban or that she likes Josh Groban more than she likes you. In such cases, it is often wise to reword the sentence.

who and whom?

In all but the most formal English, you can use *who* in any position in a sentence except after a preposition, when you must use *whom*: *the man who spoke to you, the man who you spoke to* but *the man to whom you spoke.* Similarly *for whom, with whom, by whom, than whom*, etc.

Words often confused or misused

accept = to take, believe, agree to	**except** = not including
adverse = bad, unfavourable	**averse** = not liking, against
advice = guidance	**advise** = to give advice
affect = to influence, change, concern	**effect** = (noun) result, consequence, outcome; (verb) to cause, bring about, carry out
alternate = one after the other	**alternative** = different
appraise = to form an opinion about	**apprise** = to tell

on behalf of = for	**on the part of** = by

casual, causal: Have you written the right word?

censor = person who checks acceptability of films, etc	**censure** = blame

choose = to select	**chose** = past tense of **choose**

coarse = rough, rude	**course** = part of meal, route of river, golf area **of course**

college = place of learning	**collage** = type of picture

complacent = not concerned	**complaisant** = happy to comply

complaint, compliant: Have you written the right word?

compliment = (noun) praise; (verb) to give praise	**complement** = (noun) something that goes well with something else, full number; (verb) to go well with, make complete

comprise: While increasingly common, *comprise of* is not yet generally accepted as correct: *Great Britain comprises England, Scotland and Wales*, not *Great Britain is comprised of England, Scotland and Wales*. The phrase *consists of* is correct, though.

contemptible = worthy of contempt	**contemptuous** = showing contempt

continual = happening repeatedly	**continuous** = without a break

council = body of officials, committee	**counsel** = (noun) advice, lawyer in court; (verb) to advise, warn

councillor = member of council (but members of some advice-giving councils are called **counsellors**)	**counsellor** = adviser

credible = believable	**creditable** = worthy of praise

currant = type of fruit	**current** = (adjective) valid or happening at the present time; (noun) flow of water, air or electricity
desert = (noun) place with few plants; (verb) to leave	**dessert** = part of meal
device = tool, means of doing something	**devise** = to create
diary, dairy: Have you written the correct word?	
discomfort = slight pain	**discomfit** = to embarrass or disconcert
discreet = tactful	**discrete** = separate
distinct = clear	**distinctive** = characteristic
draft = rough version, bank payment order	**draught** = current of air, minimum depth of water for ships, amount drunk
elicit = to get information, etc	**illicit** = unlawful, not allowed
eligible = suitable, qualified	**illegible** = unreadable
eminent = distinguished, important	**imminent** = about to happen
ensure = to make sure	**insure** = to take out insurance
envelop = to surround or cover	**envelope** = cover for a letter
equable = calm	**equitable** = fair
fatal = causing death	**fateful** = of great importance
flaunt = to show off	**flout** = to ignore or break (rules)
fortunate = lucky	**fortuitous** = happening by chance
imply = to suggest	**infer** = to form an opinion; *also* to suggest (though many people do not approve of this use of the word)

its = of it	**it's** = it is *or* it has
judicial = relating to judges	**judicious** = wise
licence = (noun) paper giving permission	**license** = (verb) to give permission to

literally: Only use this if you really mean 'exactly what is meant by the following word or words'.

loose = not tight	**lose** = (verb) to no longer have something
manifold = of many kinds	**manifest** = clear
mitigate = to lessen the seriousness of	**militate** = to act (against)
nought = zero	**naught** = nothing: *The plan came to naught.*
paramount = most important	**tantamount** = equal (to)
passed = (verb) *he passed the house, passed the test, passed the ball.*	**past** = (preposition) *he went past the house*; (noun) *happened in the past*; (adjective) gone by, before now
practice = (noun) doing something regularly, doctor's work	**practise** = (verb) to do something regularly so as to get better
precede = to go before	**proceed** = to begin or continue with an activity
precipitate = hasty	**precipitous** = steep
principal = (adjective) main, most important; (noun) chief person, head	**principle** = general rule, belief, morality
purposefully = with a purpose	**purposely** = deliberately, on purpose
refute = to prove (something) wrong	**deny** = to say that something is wrong

so therefore: Both these words mean the same thing, so use one or the other but not the two together.

stationary = not moving	**stationery** = paper, pens, etc
there = not here	**their** = of them **they're** = they are
theirs = of them	**there's** = there is
to = in the direction of, towards	**too** = also, excessively **two** = 1 + 1
wave = (verb) to move from side to side; (noun) wave of water, air, sound, etc	**waive** = not ask for
whose = of whom	**who's** = who is
your = of you	**you're** = you are

Words often misspelt

Do not rely on spellcheckers. A spellchecker can only tell you whether or not a word you have typed is in its vocabulary file. If you type in *posible* or *possable* for *possible*, your spellchecker will correct the spelling error or flag it up for you to correct. But if you type *of coarse* when you should have typed *of course*, the spellchecker will not regard that as an error, because *coarse* is an English word and *of coarse* is a perfectly possible sequence of words (e.g. *Cover the seeds with a layer of coarse sand*). The same is true for some of the commonest spelling errors in English such as *it's* for *its*, *their* for *there*, *who's* for *whose*.

Words with double letters often wrongly spelt with a single letter

abbreviation, accommodation, accompany, accomplish, account, accumulate, accurate, accuse, accustomed (note also: *acknowledge, acquaint, acquire*), *additional, address, affect, afford, aggravate, aggressive, allegation, allege, alleviate, allocate, announce, annoy, annual, appalling, apparent, appeal, appear, apply, appreciate, approach, appropriate, approve, approximate, arrange, assemble, assistance, associate, assume, assumption, assure, attach, attention, attitude, attraction*

collaborate, collapse, colleague, collect, college, collide, command, commence, comment, commercial, commitment, committee, connect, correct, corroborate

deterrent, different, difficult, disappear, disappoint, disapprove, dissatisfied, dissuade

effect, efficient, effort, embarrassed, exaggerate

horrific, horrified, horror

illegal, illegible, illogical, illustrate, immediate, immense, immigrant, immoral, innocent, irrational, irrelevant, irritate

marvellous

necessary, necessity

occasion, occupy, occur, occurrence, offend, offer, official, opportunity, oppose

possess, possible

recommend, recurring, recurrence, referral, regrettable, remittance

sufficient, suppose

terrible, terrific, terrified

unforgettable, unnatural, unnecessary

Words with single letters often wrongly spelt with a double letter

abandoned, abolish, abolition, abominable, abysmal, accumulate, accurate, across, adequate, admit, adolescent, advantage, advertise, agree, almost, already, altogether, amount, anoint, apart, apology

benefit

career, collaborate, colossal

disappear, disappoint, disapprove

fulfil

harassed

inaccurate, inept

necessary, necessity

omit, omission

probable, profit

recommend, recur, recurrence, refer, referee, reference, referral, require (compare *acquire*)

similar, similarity, skilful

terrific, terrifying, tomorrow

unusual, until

wilful

-able or -ible?

- **-able:** *abominable, adorable, advisable, believable, changeable, culpable, debatable, detectable, excusable, formidable, inevitable, inexcusable, inexplicable, liable, manageable, memorable, negotiable, notable, noticeable, preferable, preventable, probable, regrettable, reliable, unbelievable, undeniable, unforgettable, unforgivable, valuable*

- **-ible:** *accessible, collapsible, compatible, credible, discernible, eligible, feasible, flexible, gullible, horrible, illegible, incomprehensible, incontrovertible, inedible, irresponsible, negligible, ostensible, plausible, possible, responsible, reversible, sensible, susceptible, tangible, terrible, visible*

-ance or -ence, -ant or -ent?

- **-an-:** *acceptance, acquaintance, allowance, annoyance, appearance, appliance, assistance, assurance, attendant, balance, brilliant, circumstances, distance, exorbitant, extravagant, fragrant, guidance, hindrance, ignorant, instance, irrelevant, maintenance, nuisance, performance, pleasant, preponderance, redundancy, relevant, reluctant, remittance, resemblance, resistance, semblance, significance, substance, tolerance, vacancy, vigilance*

- **-en-:** *abhorrent, coincidence, competent, complacent, condolences, confident, consequences, consistent, convenient, correspondence, deterrent, different, diligence, equivalent, excellence, existence, experience, incident, inconsistency, inconvenience, independence, indulgence, influence, insistence, intelligent, interference, licence, negligence, occurrence, patience, permanent, persistent, preference, presence, prevalent, prudent, reference, resident, sufficient, tendency*

*dependa*nt = (noun) person who depends on someone else

dependent = (adjective) depending on something

independent (noun and adjective)

-ise or -ize?

Most words can be spelt with -*s*- or -*z*- (e.g. *equalise* or *equalize*), but some only with -*s*- and one only with -*z*-:

- **only -s-:** *advise, apprise, arise, chastise, circumcise, comprise, compromise, despise, devise, disguise, excise, exercise, franchise, improvise, incise, revise, supervise, surmise, surprise, televise*

- **only -z-:** *capsize*

-ly

Many adverbs need a double *l*: *accidentally, actually, awfully, basically, critically, finally, fully, normally, really, politically, practically, specifically, usually, wholly*

But note: *publicly, duly, truly, unduly*

Words that end in *-or* and *-ar*, not *-er*

- **-or:** *accelerator, administrator, advisor* (or *adviser*), *ancestor, arbitrator, author, benefactor, calculator, chancellor, collaborator, collector, commentator, contractor, councillor, counsellor, creator, creditor, decorator, director, doctor, donor, editor, governor, guarantor, illustrator, impostor, indicator, instructor, investor, mayor, objector, operator, predecessor, proprietor, processor, protector, radiator, rector, refrigerator, solicitor, sponsor, surveyor, ventilator, visitor*

- **-ar:** *beggar, burglar, bursar, liar, pedlar, registrar, scholar, vicar*

Plurals of words ending in *-o*

Nouns that end in *-o* mostly follow the regular rule for forming plurals and just add *-s*: *avocados, cameos, cellos, cuckoos,* etc

With some nouns that end in *-o*, there is a choice between adding *-s* and *-es*: e.g. *banjos* or *banjoes, cargoes/cargos, ghettos/ghettoes, grottoes/grottos, haloes/halos, innuendoes/innuendos, lassos/lassoes, mangoes/mangos, mementoes/mementos, mosquitoes/mosquitos, mottoes/mottos, volcanoes/volcanos, zeros/zeroes*

Some nouns always add *-es* in the plural: *buffaloes, echoes, embargoes, goes, heroes, Negroes, noes, potatoes, tomatoes, tornadoes, torpedoes, vetoes*

Words to watch

allege, almighty, almost, a lot, already, all right, also, although, altogether, always, argument, arbitrary, attach

conceited, deceit but *receipt*

defence, offence but *defensive, offensive*; *detach* but *dispatch*; *desperate, definitely*; *democracy* but *hypocrisy*

exceed, exciting, extraordinary

gauge, gauze

have: should **have**, must **have**, could **have**, etc, not *should of*, etc

laid, paid, said; *liaison*

medicine, messenger, minuscule, miscellaneous

parliament, passenger; *precede* but *proceed, succeed*; *procedure*; *privilege, pronunciation*

recognise

separate, several, surprise